PIRANESI

PIRANESI

NICHOLAS PENNY

BLOOMSBURY BOOKS
LONDON

(frontispiece)
Joseph NOLLEKENS
Giovanni Battista Piranesi
Rome, Accademia di San Luca.
Marble 57 cm. high.

This bust by Nollekens, formerly attributed to Giuseppe Angelini, was recently recognized by John Wilton-Ely. It probably dates from the late 1760s, towards the end of Nollekens's stay in Rome, where he had been highly active as a restorer and copier and as a dealer in antiquities.

ACKNOWLEDGEMENTS

I am most grateful to Charles Hope for encouraging me to write this book and to many friends with whom I have discussed its contents, especially Roger Jones, Roger Ling, Suzy Bulters, Tom Rasmussen and Francis and Larissa Haskell. My wife, despite formidable distractions, gave me invaluable assistance when I was writing the first draft and Robert Oresko far surpassed the duties of the most scrupulous editor in the improvements which he made to the typescript. Special thanks are also due to Josephine Abbott of the Ashmolean Museum for her help in obtaining photographs. My greatest debt is to David Udy, from whom I have learnt so much about both Piranesi and his period.

I must also thank the following for their kind assistance in providing photographs: Accademia di San Luca, Rome; Ashmolean Museum, Oxford; Avery Architectural Library, Columbia University, New York; British Library, London; British Museum, London; Courtauld Institute, London; Hermitage Museum, Leningrad; John Rylands University Library of Manchester, Manchester; La Société des Architectes Diplômés par le Gouvernement, Paris; Musée de Dunkerque, Dunkerque; National Gallery of Scotland, Edinburgh; National Monuments Record, Royal Commission on Historical Monuments, London; Palazzo Farnese, Rome; Pierpont Morgan Library, New York; Rijksmuseum, Amsterdam; Royal Institute of British Architects, London; Sir John Soane's Museum, London; Städelsches Kunstinstitut, Frankfurt-am-Main; Victoria and Albert Museum, London; Wellington Museum, Apsley House, London; Alinari, Florence; Ets. J. Bulloz, Paris; A. C. Cooper, London; *Country Life*, London.

For David

This edition published 1988 by
Bloomsbury Books an imprint of
Godfrey Cave Associates Limited
42 Bloomsbury Street, London WC1B 3QJ
under license from Minotaur Publishing Co Ltd

ISBN 1 870630 50 5

Printed in Yugoslavia

Giovanni Battista Piranesi

IT IS USUAL, and quite correct, to describe Piranesi as a great etcher and as a great draughtsman. But he was also an architect and that is how he would have wished us to think of him. It is true that he built very little; but in his age it was easier than it has ever been, before or since, to display architectural genius without building. This was achieved through the painting or etching of architectural views, through archaeology, through the design of ephemeral theatrical architecture and through painted architecture for interior decoration. Piranesi engaged in all these activities, although chiefly in the first two, and brief consideration of them provides a useful introduction to his art.

In eighteenth-century Italy there was a market, far more extensive than any that had existed earlier, for easel paintings or, as Piranesi discovered, etchings of architectural subjects. These were chiefly accurate views of what had been built. Photography may encourage us to think of the creation of such views as 'mechanical', and this was also the official view of art theorists in the eighteenth century, but the picture-buying public clearly held topographical artists in high esteem, and there were other types of architectural pictures, produced by the same artists, which could never have been considered as mechanical, such as the impossibly extravagant projects for new buildings and fanciful medleys and the reconstructions of ancient ruins of the sort which play an important part in Piranesi's art.

Just as we need to escape from the idea of the post-card in order to appreciate the art of the eighteenth-century view-painter, so we need to escape from the twentieth-century idea of archaeology if we are to appreciate the eighteenth-century passion for anti-quity. Archaeology was not then the work of experts, published for the benefit of other experts in learned journals, occasionally leading to the exhibition of exotic treasure which captured the popular imagina-tion. In the eighteenth century the imagination of educated Europeans was truly engaged by the archae-ologists whose findings affected their way of life by providing, for instance, new models for the columns of their porticoes, the stucco of their ceilings and the bronze statuettes on their chimneypieces. The work of the archaeologist not only inspired the architect, it also provided, as was the case with Piranesi, an outlet for the frustrated architect's imagination and a means to advertise his erudition to potential patrons.

There were other important outlets for the budding architect or the architect *manqué*: splendid sham architecture, half-painted, half-carpentry, was then essential for operas, oratorios, funerals and firework displays and the inventors of such spectacles were as highly esteemed as the composers and pyrotechnicians. In addition, in southern Europe especially during the seventeenth and eighteenth centuries, the extensive and magnificent interiors of great palaces and churches were further extended by an even more magnificent painted architecture of airy colonnades, cloud-filled vaults and suites of courtyards. Such work often provided the setting for allegorical, historical and pastoral narratives, but the painting of the architecture itself was valued quite as much as the central composition it was designed to frame. As a young man Piranesi seems to have been involved in some scenogra-phic enterprises (Plate 11), and, at the end of his life, although not a painter, he designed interior decoration of an architectural character (Plate 83). Above all he was brought up in Venice, a city where even the real architecture appears to be a scene-painter's trick.

Giovanni Battista Piranesi was born at Mogliano in the Veneto in 1720, the son of a Venetian mason builder. It was intended that he should be an architect and he was apprenticed briefly to his maternal uncle, Matteo Lucchesi, the leading hydraulics engineer in Venice, who probably provided a sound training in masonry construction, and equally briefly to Giovanni Antonio Scalfarotto, the city's leading architect, who would have introduced him to the ideals of Palladian classicism. However, Piranesi's earliest surviving draw-ings have little to do with the practical world of stone and mortar. A sheet in the British Museum showing two courtyards (Plate 1) is typical of such works, an accomplished exercise in perspective in which the architecture is purely scenographic. It probably reflects a third brief spell of training in Venice under Carlo Zucchi, etcher, seal-engraver and author of a treatise on perspective. The drawing also reminds us that Pira-nesi's early biographers connect him with the Bibiena family (fig. 2) and with the Valeriani brothers, leading scenographic designers of the period.

The important art of scene-painting and stage

fig. 1 Studio of Filippo JUVARRA
Hall with a Staircase
London, Royal Institute of British Architects.
Pen, brown ink and wash 20·3 × 16·6 cm.

This idea for extravagant stage architecture, executed in about 1730, is almost as bold in conception as Piranesi's later sketches of fantastic architecture and the drawing style, although different, is as spontaneous. The arches springing in several directions from a central group of columns through which we glimpse flights of stairs and palatial halls was a popular compositional device in drawings of this sort, later taken up by Piranesi (Plate 43).

fig. 2 Giuseppe GALLI-BIBIENA
Architetture e Prospettive, plate four
Engraving by Johann Andreas Pfeffel
50 × 32·5 cm. c.1740.

Piranesi was said by Legrand to have actually studied under Ferdinando Galli-Bibiena, but this is most improbable. Piranesi must however have known Ferdinando's published works on perspective and also the *Architetture e Prospettive* by Ferdinando's son and successor as theatrical engineer and designer at the imperial court in Vienna, Giuseppe. The title of Piranesi's first publication, the *Prima parte di architettura e prospettive*, alone suggests a debt to Giuseppe's book, published only three years earlier, in Augsburg in 1740. In this plate the artist's text, or rather his pretext, is Christ led by soldiers up the staircase of the Jewish Temple. Piranesi never treated biblical subject matter nor indeed any explicit narrative, but the figures in his early plates are equally small in relation to the architecture as those in this print.

construction had been transformed at the close of the seventeenth century by the greatest of the Bibiena family, Ferdinando Galli-Bibiena, who was said to have invented and who certainly perfected and popularized *scene vedute in angolo*, oblique perspective views, in his sets. This idea was perhaps devised in response to the difficulty of creating in small theatres an illusion of depth by means of a central clearing in the stage architecture. An orthodox 'centralized' recession, after all, could only work for those of the audience opposite the stage. Piranesi's oblique presentation of the two courtyards is certainly in the Galli-Bibiena tradition, and although very few of his later works look so like stage designs as does the British Museum sheet, they often utilize the same compositional devices. In this drawing no element is parallel to the picture plane. Thus, instead of a lucid sequence, there is a complex interpenetration of spaces, and, instead of a uniform progression towards a central vanishing point, there are crossing diagonals and opposing temptations for the eye.

The British Museum drawing seems likely to date from around 1740, the year in which Piranesi went to Rome as a draughtsman in the ambassadorial train sent by the Venetian senate to pay respects to the new pope, Benedict XIV. Certainly the architecture is not yet Roman in character. Piranesi stayed in Rome and published a series of twelve etchings there in the summer of 1743, entitled *Prima parte di architettura e prospettive*, the work of a young architect attempting to attract attention by a display of learned and ambitious ideas. In at least one etching (Plate 2) the architecture is still purely scenographic and the plan has not been considered from any practical point of view. The etching is described as 'loco magnifico d'architettura' in 1743, but in 1750, when it was republished, a text was added informing us that the steps lead to various floors, although it is impossible to see how, and stating that the rotunda is for 'theatrical representations', for which it would be ludicrously unsuitable. The majority of the twelve etchings of 1743, however, are more than splendid perspectives. Some show the ruins of ancient Roman buildings, and most of the etchings either reconstruct these ruins or are projects clearly inspired by them.

As has already been mentioned, Piranesi, before travelling to Rome, was briefly apprenticed to Scalfarotto. This architect would certainly have encouraged his pupils to emulate the ancients, to avoid the extravagant ornamentation of modern architecture and to revere Palladio. Piranesi referred dutifully to the 'immortal' Palladio in the dedicatory epistle to the *Prima parte* etchings and his conception of the ancient Temple of Vesta (Plate 3) was influenced by the Pantheon, the building which inspired Scalfarotto's Church of San Simeone Piccolo in Venice. Although the young Piranesi did take a few idiosyncratic ideas from Fischer von Erlach, the ornament for the Temple of Vesta is typically restrained, or, as a Palladian would have said, 'correct'. All the same Piranesi's idea is extravagant in one way: this 'pantheon' is so inflated that an open tempietto, where the virgin priestesses preserve their sacred fire, is erected inside it. This idea perhaps originated in ephemeral architecture rather than in archaeology, for since the mid-sixteenth century the climax of the elaborate pomp of prestigious obsequies was an architectural catafalque involving a baldachin of candles raised on columns above the remains of the deceased and ranged round with statues. Placed beneath the dome of a great church these were virtually buildings within buildings and perhaps helped Piranesi to conceive of the idea of this temple within a temple. This idea of wrapping one building around another was typical of the baroque imagination, and Piranesi's etching has reminded one scholar of Carlo Fontana's project for building a church *inside* the Colosseum.

Whatever promise we may find in the *Prima parte* designs they do not seem to have proved a successful advertisement for Piranesi's qualifications as an architect. He was not taken up by a great patron, and it must have been clear to him that the building activity in

Rome during the 1730s, which saw the erection of, among other works, the façades of San Giovanni in Laterano and Santa Maria Maggiore, the two most important churches in the city after St. Peter's, would not be renewed in the 1740s. The wealth in Rome seemed more than ever to be in the pockets of the German, French and English visitors, the last being increasingly conspicuous. In 1744 Piranesi returned to Venice where it is supposed that he worked in Giambattista Tiepolo's studio. He was back in Rome in 1745, but there is an impressive body of work which survives from that Venetian stay or was at least inspired by it. Venice was, of course, unrivalled at that date by any other city as an artistic centre, and it was far fuller of native talent than Rome. The names of Piazetta, Ricci, Guardi, Canaletto, Longhi and Tiepolo come more easily to mind than do the names of any contemporary Roman artists.

Certainly dating from his brief Venetian trip are Piranesi's designs for frames and sconces and for a ceremonial gondola or *bissona*, this last being a sparkling rococo soufflé of foam, shells, scrolls and dolphins (Plate 10). There is also a drawing in Paris, probably dating from this period, which suggests a connection with the theatre, for it is framed by a sort of proscenium arch and includes what is certainly stage machinery (Plate 11). But the most remarkable of Piranesi's Venetian works are the *Grotteschi* etchings, in which the festivity is qualified by a certain elegaic and even sinister note (Plates 12 and 13).

The *Grotteschi* are clearly related to Giambattista Tiepolo's series, the *Varii capricci* and the *Scherzi di fantasia*. Tiepolo's mysterious etchings illustrate no known text and have no recognizable narrative meaning. Many of them include ruins and skeletons which suggest comparisons with earlier allegories of worldly vanity. They are, however, not simple allegories, but are full of meanings of the kind which cannot be translated into words (fig. 3). Piranesi's *Grotteschi* are similarly mysterious, although, since the individual figures are less important, one is not even tempted to look for a narrative meaning. A litter of crumbling antiques, bones and snakes mingled with rococo shells, scrolls and dolphins adorns a pleasant landscape. The imagery seems designed to stimulate contradictory moods and trains of association in a way which is more genuinely analogous to music than much art that claims to be musical.

It was not from these perplexing works of fantasy, however, that Piranesi was to achieve his fame and fortune, but through the far more mundane task of recording the popular tourist sights of Rome. These in their way were also Venetian in inspiration. By the time he left Rome in 1744 Piranesi, as we have noted, must have realized that the real wealth in Rome belonged to foreign visitors. Prints of the sights of Rome had been made for these travellers for two centuries, and some of

fig. 3 Giambattista TIEPOLO
Scherzi di fantasia, number five: *Seated Magician Regarding Animal Skulls, with Other Figures and an Altar*
Etching 22·5 × 17·8 cm.

This plate belongs to a series of fourteen etchings, *Scherzi di fantasia*, first published as a group in 1775 but certainly executed earlier. The clear influence of these works in Piranesi's *Grotteschi* (Plates 12 and 13) indicates that they should be dated no later than the mid-1740s when Piranesi was in Venice.

them, those made in the first years of the eighteenth century by Specchi, for instance, were of a very high quality. But it was in Venice, a city which had gone further than any other in Italy to encourage tourism, that a really large scale trade was first developed in souvenir prints of a high quality, 'curious stamps of the several edifices which are most famous for their beauty or magnificence', as Joseph Addison described them in 1705. Addison had Carlevaris's 104 etched views of 1703 in mind. In the early 1740s Marieschi's etchings of the city appeared and so did the second series of Visentini's engravings after Canaletto. Their success would have been noted by Piranesi, who, on his return to Rome in 1745, no longer supported by an allowance from his father but acting as an agent for Wagner, the Venetian print-seller, began his career as a topographical artist.

Piranesi's first works of this type were a series of some forty-eight small etched views of famous Roman sights,

ancient and modern, which were bound into guidebooks by the Roman print-seller Fausto Amidei, who also employed a number of French artists. Thirty-six of Piranesi's etchings were actually published in 1745, but although a few, rather puzzlingly, appear in a copy of a book published as early as 1741, they were perhaps bound into this copy at a later date. These views were hack work and we need not wonder that they vary greatly in quality. But at their best, when too much detail was not needed, they possess the character of brisk sketches, effortlessly evocative of light and atmosphere and very free in their technique (Plate 14). In comparison the *Prima parte* etchings appear laboured and tentative, but freedom and confidence are of course more easily achieved on the small scale of these views.

Larger than these little etchings, although still small especially by his later standards, is a series which Piranesi published in 1748 with the title *Antichità romane de' tempi della republica e de' primi imperatori*, but which he later renamed *Alcune vedute di archi trionfali ed altri monumenti* (Plates 15 and 16). These display all the qualities of the smaller and earlier works but are of a more consistent standard and are more cleverly, although not always securely, composed, with a varied choice of viewpoints and framing devices, some of which reflect perhaps an awareness of Canaletto's etchings, which may well have been published in Venice during Piranesi's stay there.

By 1748 Piranesi had already started a series of much more ambitious topographical prints, the celebrated *Vedute di Roma* (Plates 17–32, 60–63, 71). He was to continue to produce these views of Rome until his death, at which date there were 133 plates in the series. A quarter of these were published in 1751 by Bouchard, the French bookseller on the Corso, and they quickly established the artist's fame, being more attractive, larger and more informative than rival prints of the city. Piranesi's intention was at first essentially the same as Canaletto's in his paintings of Venice, or Panini's in his views, as distinct from his caprices, of Rome (fig. 4) and as Claude-Joseph Vernet's in his paintings of the ports of France, to list only a few of the remarkable topographical achievements of the eighteenth century. It was, quite simply, to make as attractive a picture as was compatible with providing accurate visual information. But in the later plates, and especially after 1760, Piranesi was concerned to achieve more than this. Some of his views, especially those of Tivoli and its environs (Plates 60–63), which can in fact be considered separately, are truly sublime. Other views however, especially some of the very last, are invested with a rather specious melodrama and are carelessly composed. As a general rule the disappointing examples of the late *Vedute* show Renaissance and baroque Rome rather than the antique. It was the relics of a dead civilization which gave life to the imagination of the old Piranesi.

fig. 4 Giovanni Paolo PANINI
*View of the Spanish Embassy in Piazza di Spagna,
Rome, Showing Festivities for the Ratification of the
Treaty of Vienna*
London, Apsley House, Wellington Museum.
Oil on canvas 43·8 × 97·5 cm.

It was view-paintings such as this one by
Panini, just as much as earlier etchings, which
Piranesi strove to emulate in his large *Vedute di
Roma.* A great many pictures of this type, a
high percentage of Canaletto's for example
and Panini's large painting of the Piazza
Navona in the Musée du Louvre, record
festivals with all their ephemeral decor as well
as the durable architecture. In this painting
there is a neat temple, possibly dedicated to
Peace and derived from Bramante's San Pietro
in Montorio, on top of a 'mountain' upon
which mythological figures enact an
appropriate allegory. Some of Piranesi's early
architectural ideas are best understood as
equivalents to this sort of festive architecture
rather than as projects for solid buildings.

In the early *Vedute* the street life is usually convinc-
ing. There are hay-wagons and fashionable coaches;
chair-makers, wheelwrights and stall-keepers, as well as
the beggars at the street corners and the *milordi*
clustered around a guide; and the common women put
up washing whilst ladies promenade in their pannier
skirts; rags and riches picturesquely but not painfully
juxtaposed. In the later work, however, beggars appear
to have overrun the city and prowl amid the debris
waving dislocated arms in desperate conversation with
deaf companions; the feminine element in the popula-
tion declines steeply; the tourists are not merely
pleased, but staggered by what they see; the chiaroscuro increases and can be quite menacing; the sky
darkens, troubled by deep parallel grooves; and there is
also less of the sky because the viewpoint tends to be
closer and lower, or, more rarely, much higher, so that
buildings occupy more of the print and are often cut by
its edges.

Piranesi cannot have devoted all his attention to
topography during the second half of the 1740s for he
published in 1750 a collection of etchings entitled *Opere
varie.* This collection included the *Grotteschi*, which at
least originated in the mid-1740s and have been
mentioned already, and the 1743 *Prima parte*, with some
additions. One addition to the *Prima parte*, surely
originally intended for a *seconda parte*, is a *capriccio* of
ruins entitled *Vestiggi d'antichi edifici* (*Remains of Ancient
Buildings*), only slightly less tentative in the handling
than the similar views of ruins in the original *Prima parte*
(Plates 6 and 7). Like many of Panini's souvenir pieces
this is not an exercise in accurate topography, for
instead an accurately drawn antique item, in this case
the celebrated 'bath' of Marcus Agrippa, was translated into a fanciful setting. In Piranesi's mature works
the foreground masonry is less woolly, the perspective
of the temple's entablature more confidently drawn,
the disparities of scale more deliberately exploited and
the weak tree stump replaced by vigorous, if crippled,
vegetation. But hints of future power are sure enough in
the *Opere varie*, especially in the gloomy foreground with
its architectural fragments arranged dramatically in
contrasting shapes and at contrasting angles.

The *Opere varie* also include works in the manner of
the Temple of Vesta interior (Plate 3), although the
artist's inventions were more daring at this point.
Indeed, he was never bolder than in his view of a
Magnificent Port (Plate 33), in which the juxtaposition of
each piece of architecture was brilliantly calculated to
play a part in a drama of contrasted axes. The huge
arch in the centre of the foreground thrusts forward to
the right, for instance, but the movement is countered
by the steps rushing back into space and by the curve of
the colossal building behind. 'He piles palaces on
bridges, and temples on palaces, and scales Heaven
with mountains of edifices', exclaimed Horace Wal-

fig. 5 Sarcophagus of Cecilia Metella
Rome, Palazzo Farnese. 40 B.C. Marble.

Piranesi depicted this once-celebrated
sarcophagus in the third volume of *Antichità
romane* in plate fifty-two and illustrated the
broken state in which it was discovered in the
Metella mausoleum. Although he expressed
some concern that the ornamentation might
be too capricious and grotesque to be proper,
he nevertheless used it as the starting point for
far more capricious and grotesque inventions
of his own (Plates 34 and 43).

pole. But he added: 'What labour and thought both in
his rashness and details'. The smoke from the altar of
Neptune was a useful expedient enabling Piranesi to
escape the problem of an arch springing over our heads
and out of the composition. One might also suppose it
to have been a scene-painter's trick to hide the fact that
Piranesi had not thought about how the building
would continue. This is not so. The buildings are
presented in a manner which frustrates any easy
understanding of their plan, but which was, nevertheless, worked out laboriously.

Whereas the decoration of the *Prima parte* Temple of
Vesta (Plate 3) was tamely 'correct', in the *Magnificent
Port* (Plate 33) we have ornament based upon, but not
always imitating exactly, the more barbaric and exotic
of Roman ornaments. The Romans had rostral
columns which Piranesi depicted, but along with a

rostral frieze of his own invention. The Romans had
obelisks and columns adorned with spiral relief
sculpture, but the fluted obelisk on the right of the
Magnificent Port, which passes through a block with
an oval relief and rostral appendages and which
becomes a tapering storiated column, is a fantastic
invention. Most bizarre of all is the foreground pier
with its massive trophy jammed into the corbelled
ledge, which supports the truncated pyramid, and the
fluted shaft capped by the urn and flag. Such
concoctions look forward to Piranesi's later experi-
ments with brutal combinations of disparate ornamental elements.

However boldly he displayed his taste in such designs
as the *Magnificent Port*, Piranesi did not yet have the
critical courage to defend his taste. In one of his later
archaeological publications, he wrote, *à propos* the
'capricciosi ornamenti a grottesci' on the sarcophagus
of Cecilia Metella (fig. 5), that such decoration is
acceptable on a tomb, but that Vitruvius was right to
disapprove of it on public buildings. Yet despite this
Piranesi covered the public buildings of his port with
ornaments far more grotesque than those on the
Metella sarcophagus.

Another point to be made about the *Magnificent Port*
etching is that the figures cannot represent the ancients
for whom and by whom the building was, we are to

suppose, designed. The sepulchral urns set in niches of the port wall contain the ashes of worthy captains killed in combat, but they are capacious enough for the remains of dozens of the men depicted here. Nor would it be possible for men of such small stature to reach the mooring rings, even supposing they could lift the ropes. After the diminutive priestesses of his Temple of Vesta Piranesi did not people his views with individuals easily identifiable as ancients, but only depicted the stupendous relics of their superhuman achievements. And ruin has already set in. On the far right the battle between vegetation and masonry, a constant theme in Piranesi's work, has commenced.

Perhaps also published in 1750, and certainly not later, were Piranesi's *Invenzioni capric di carceri*, which were entirely reworked and republished with additional plates under the new title *Carceri d'invenzione* just over a decade later (Plates 35-42). These are the 'prison' etchings for which Piranesi is now most famous. This fame, however, was certainly not instantaneous and seems in fact to have been largely posthumous. Preparatory drawings survive which provide astonishing evidence of the violence with which the artist hurled down his ideas. This violence was retained in the plates, and, indeed, one would not suppose from the apparent spontaneity of the results that Piranesi had made any preparatory drawings at all. None of this spontaneity was lost in the *Carceri d'invenzione*, in which there are considerable changes which make the plates grimmer and darker and the compositions much stronger. But mistakes in perspective were not corrected in this second edition, and one's feeling that the artist has attacked the plate is, if anything, enhanced. The 'labour and thought' which Walpole admired is here deliberately invisible.

Flights of stairs in the *Carceri* etchings always impress one as a series of parallel dashes before they are seen as steps. Each of the smaller lines also has an independent life. They tremble indecisively in some areas and in others are activated like iron filings caught in a magnetic field, for example around the knotted rope and chains of the frontispiece (Plates 35 and 36). Here was compensation indeed for the control Piranesi exercised over the etching needle in his other works. His style is an equivalent in etching to the extraordinary, almost lightning-like, brushwork of Alessandro Magnasco (fig. 6), the subjects of whose paintings are frequently as menacing as those of the *Carceri*.

Once seen the *Carceri* series will not be forgotten easily; but the individual plates tend to get mixed up in the memory. Timbers crossing in a busy diagonal pattern and sudden openings into complicated depths, through, over and under the massive ruined piers and arches out of which the 'prisons' are improvised — such effects are common to most of the series. There are some arresting details: broken garlands of chain which resemble hanged vermin; trophies of a plumed helmet,

shields, a club and chains which resemble crouching animals; carved heads gripping iron rings with their teeth, prisoners' heads and not, as one at first supposes, lions' heads. These are focused moments in a confused dream, confused because there is no narrative to follow, because it is never clear what exactly the figures are doing and because it is not even at all clear what manner of prisons these are.

In the fourteenth plate (Plate 40) there are bars and spiked instruments and, hanging on the right, a cage. But, although some Iago may be supposed to rot inside the cage, the pulley beside it and the grim apparatus below do not impress one as likely to be still in use. Moreover, both the cage and the spikes are in fact absent from the first state of the etching (Plate 39). In some plates there are groups of chained men. Some prisoners slink behind warders. But they are never confined to dungeons and are, in most cases, free to wander up zigzag and corkscrew stairs and across wooden galleries, there to survey through arches, other arches and, through festoons of rope and past timber bridges, other timber bridges.

In the second, and entirely transformed, state of the sixteenth plate (Plate 42) and also in plates two (Plate 37) and five, which were entirely new additions to the original set, Piranesi added some specificity to his scenes. These prisons are all clearly located in, or at least loaded with allusions to, antiquity. The second plate (Plate 37), for instance, contains the effigies and names of notable victims of Nero's persecutions. Is this a public torture display put on by that tyrant for the edification of the Roman mob? The narrative is far from clear. The composition is also too crowded, so that the effect of the jagged timber fingers above the prisoner on his rack, an explosion in the centre of the composition, loses a good deal of its impact.

The learned references in these two plates, only fully tracked down in an article of 1971 by Silvia Stewart, remind us that between the first and second editions of the *Carceri* Piranesi had established himself as one of the most eminent Roman archaeologists and antiquarians. His *Antichità romane* came out in four volumes in 1756 and was an altogether more ambitious work than the set of views, *Antichità romane de' tempi della republica e de' primi imperatori*, published in 1748. The 1756 *Antichità romane* volumes were preceded by a small publication on the trophies of the Capitoline, *Trofei di Ottaviano Augusto*. In 1761, the same year as the revised *Carceri*, he published a study of Roman aqueducts and plumbing, *Le rovine del Castello dell' Acqua Giulia*, and also *Lapides Capitolini*, prints of inscribed tablets in the Capitoline.

Then, in 1762, he published the *Campus Martius*, dedicated to Robert Adam, and his *Discrezione e disegno dell' emissario del Lago Albano*, and, two years later, the *Antichità d'Albano e di Castel Gandolfo* and the *Antichità di Cora*. His archaeological interests were replaced to some

Art historians, eager to trace the aesthetic
ancestry of Piranesi's prison etchings, the
Carceri (Plates 35–42), have rightly related
them to a minor tradition in baroque stage
design, but, as Robert Oresko has suggested, it
is quite as helpful to look back to such
paintings of trials and of torture by the
Genoese painter, Alessandro Magnasco, as this
picture or its pendant, also in Frankfurt.
Magnasco's figures have limbs as long, hands
as large and a manner as desperate as
Piranesi's prisoners and the extreme freedom
of Piranesi's etching style in the *Carceri* may be
considered an equivalent to the frenetic
brushwork of Magnasco, which exerted an
important influence on such eighteenth-
century painters as Sebastiano and Marco
Ricci and Gianantonio Guardi in Piranesi's
native Venice.

extent in the late 1760s by his own architectural
activities, but later, in the mid-1770s, he produced
plates of the Columns of Trajan, Marcus Aurelius and
Antoninus Pius, and, in 1778, a collection of etchings
made during the preceding decade of candelabra, urns,
lamps, tripods and the like (*Vasi, candelabri, cippi,
sarcophagi, tripodi, lucerne, ed ornamenti antichi* . . .), many
of them in his own collection.

In the important work of the 1750s and 1760s
Piranesi must have received assistance from classical
scholars, but both the pertinacity and the sheer energy
of his field-work and the eccentricity of some of his
speculative reconstructions clearly reflect a personal
and passionate enthusiasm. The plates however are
more important than the text and the best of the plates
for the *Antichità romane* must rank, with the views of
Tivoli and its environs in the *Vedute di Roma*, among
Piranesi's greatest achievements and as one of the
greatest artistic achievements of the eighteenth century.

A view (Plate 52) of ruined mausolea on the Via
Appia outside Porta San Sebastiano is an excellent, if
little known, example of Piranesi's genius in the
Antichità romane. The unstable diamond of light left of
centre, the breaking of the front plane by the ruins
further to the right and the surprising brief opening just
before the composition closes on the far right are all
brilliant devices and work strikingly in relation to each
other. The contrasting shapes and sizes of the tall,
cactus-like ruins are also excellently calculated so that
there is a steady but not too obvious build-up of forms
from left to right, across the print. This is the direction
in which we tend to 'read' compositions. Viewed in a
mirror, that is in the reverse, which is how it was etched,
the print will appear absurdly unbalanced. Moreover,
Piranesi was also careful to place the tallest ruin in the
very centre of the print, where it was folded. In addition
movement 'across' to the right is held in tension by the

perspective of the road drawing our attention into
depth and to the left.

The best of the Tivoli *Vedute*, which date from the
1760s, do not possess such oblique and asymmetrical
complexities as those of the *Antichità romane*. The
Canopus (Plate 63), for instance, like the interior of the
Tempio della Tosse (Plate 61), is simple and symmetri-
cal, and, perhaps partly for that reason, they are easily
retained as an image by the memory. The massive
foreground fragments in the Canopus frame the figures
with such formality that the act of charity which they
perform, if such it is, is made strangely portentous. The
eye then turns to the legend and we realize with a shock
that these fragments once formed a part of the very
'canopy' beneath which the figures stand.

With the exception of the work on the storiated
columns relatively little attention is given in Piranesi's
archaeological publications to the human figure in art,
that is to statues, busts, narrative reliefs, frescoes,
painted vases or engraved gems. Piranesi was not
responsive to ideal beauty in the human form. Indeed
he was not trained to draw figures of any sort. When he
did illustrate a famous Roman bust in an initial letter
for his *Della magnificenza ed architettura de' Romani* (Plate
58) he chose the bronze *Brutus* in the Capitoline, a head
more noted for its ferocity than its classical composure.
Some might today claim that this bust is more truly
Roman than the effigies of the cultivated sensualist
Hadrian, the benevolent and philosophic Marcus
Aurelius or the cool, authoritative but infinitely
responsible and high-minded Augustus, but that was
not the usual eighteenth-century view. Even if some
connoisseurs felt that the frieze of Trajan's Column was
hardly classical in character, they would have agreed
that this emperor must have cut a dignified figure in the
original but long-since lost statue on the top. However,
in his reconstruction of the statue in his *Colonna trajana*
of c.1774 Piranesi showed Trajan standing on a globe
supported by crouching Dacian captives. The prolific
pamphleteer Cartwright observed in 1802, 'If Peronese
gives us what was the true crowning [then the ancients
lacked] either a dignity of sentiment or a chastity of
taste.' Piranesi certainly lacked chastity of taste.

If Piranesi gave relatively little attention to the
human figure in antique art then he gave plenty to the
enrichments of architecture and to ornamental carving. His feeling for the least chaste features of Roman
taste, illustrated by his love of massive trophies and
rostral columns, is always evident and perhaps blinded
him to other aspects of Roman taste. He made a row of
urns and bone houses appear ten times their actual size,
sacrificing much of their elegance and charm in the
interest of overpowering sublimity (Plate 51). Unlike
such typical neo-classical prints as those by Tatham
(fig. 7) and others, the dark etchings of the *Vasi,
candelabri, cippi*...enhance one's awareness of the vitality of the ornament, but sometimes at the expense of the

fig. 7 Charles Heathcote TATHAM
A Fragment of an Antique Frieze Found at Tivoli
Etching 10 × 35·4 cm.

This was one of the plates in Tatham's *Etchings, Representing the Best Examples of Ancient Ornamental Architecture...* (London, 1799; but some of the etchings were dated 1800). These etchings were based on drawings made by Tatham earlier in the 1790s in Italy where he acted as the agent of Henry Holland, the architect to the Prince of Wales, who was eager to obtain ideas and material for the decoration and furnishing of Carlton House. As was first demonstrated by David Udy (*The Connoisseur*, August 1971), Tatham was one of the earliest and most important promoters of the idea of rigorously applying antique prototypes to contemporary furniture and plate. His etchings, which are almost unshaded, are in deliberate contrast to Piranesi's style. Tatham praised Piranesi in the opening page of his introduction, but added that 'Fired with a genius which bad defiance to controul, and rejected with disdain the restraints of minute observation, he has sometimes sacrificed accuracy, to what he conceived the richer productions of a more fertile and exuberant mind.' Tatham suggested also that Piranesi held up for admiration some specimens of ancient sculpture which were of a 'vitiated' taste.

graceful shape. No one but Piranesi would have created a more elaborate version (Plates 43 and 47) of the already elaborate sarcophagus of Cecilia Metella (fig. 5).

Piranesi paid scant attention in his archaeological publications to the domestic side of Roman architecture and, furthermore, although he illustrated many temples, there is relatively little space given in these works to public buildings compared with that devoted to colossal mausolea and to engineering works, aqueducts, bridges, drains and fortifications. Throughout, Piranesi reveals his feeling for massive masonry construction and his understanding of the anatomy of architecture; he even described one of his plates as 'come uno spolpato scheletro', by which he perhaps meant an academic *écorché*. Ruin in his work does not only make buildings picturesque, it serves a didactic purpose at the same time by exposing the building's structure and the layers of which it is composed. He

found in his ruins the evidence of their original strength and so enhances our awareness of the forces needed to defeat such buildings.

In comparing Piranesi's depictions of ruins with those by his contemporaries one is reminded of Ruskin's distinction between landscape painters who understand the geological pressures which have given a mountain its shape and those painters who simply record that shape. Piranesi of course was trained not as a painter but as an architect. And he was the son of a mason builder. By studying half-decayed buildings Piranesi helps us to understand how they were constructed and it is entirely typical that when he paid the young British architect Robert Mylne the compliment of etching his Blackfriars Bridge, Piranesi showed it under construction rather than completed (Plate 70). Whereas other archaeologists speculated on the function of Roman buildings or on the proportional systems employed by Roman architects, Piranesi also asked how the massive blocks of the 'Capo di Bove' were lifted into place (Plate 54) and how the Via Appia was constructed.

Piranesi's earliest training was under Matteo Lucchesi, the hydraulics engineer responsible for constructing the *Murazzi*, the sea walls which girdle the Venetian lagoon, and, as Hyatt Mayor was the first to point out, the memory of these walls must account for the astonishing prints in which Piranesi exposed the foundations of the Theatre of Marcellus (Plate 55) and of the Castel Sant'Angelo, foundations which had not been excavated except by Piranesi in his imagination. His early training perhaps also explains his enthusiasm for the remarkable achievements of ancient hydraulic engineering. He was particularly excited by the tunnel which the Romans drove through the volcanic 'cup' which contains Lake Albano in order to lower the lake's level, probably to use the water for irrigation. By interrogating local peasants and bribing fishermen to penetrate the tunnel he was able to reconstruct the entire structure and he expressed his enthusiasm for the Romans' achievement by means of a magnificent lie about its scale in his view of the entrance (Plates 65 and 66).

Piranesi's archaeological activities reflected, and in

fig. 8   George DANCE the younger
Design for an Egyptian Chimneypiece of Dove Marble for the Library of Lansdowne (formerly Shelburne) House
London, Sir John Soane's Museum. Pen and coloured wash 42 × 48 cm. c.1792.

This chimneypiece, together with the less elaborate one in the 'Hall of Communication' at Dance's Stratton Park, may well reflect, as Dorothy Stroud has suggested, the influence of Piranesi's *Diverse maniere*. But like Robert Adam, who also took ideas from this book, Dance considerably chastened the fantastic inventions of Piranesi. The colossal bust of Athena was one of the treasures of the Lansdowne collection, purchased in 1771 for £104 from Piranesi's friend and associate Gavin Hamilton. The library with its grotesque wall decoration and this touch of Egyptian decor was perhaps inspired by Hadrian's Villa, from the ruins of which so many of the Lansdowne marbles were removed.

turn promoted, the new interest in the antique which is found in the second half of the eighteenth century. Of course interest had never died down and the stream of archaeological publications had never dried up since the Renaissance. In fact Piranesi's methods as an investigator were directly indebted to more modest predecessors in the early part of the eighteenth century, and he was dependent upon the authoritative late-seventeenth-century survey of Antoine Desgodetz, whose *Edifices antiques de Rome* was published in 1682 and whose work Piranesi corrected but never entirely replaced. Nevertheless there was an intensified archaeological interest in Piranesi's day, clearly manifest in the discovery of Greek architecture and the enterprising investigations of Greece, southern Italy and Asia Minor carried out by the French and English. We find evidence of this growing interest in Rome also, in the circle of Winckelmann and Mengs, in the first substantial increase of the papal collection of antiquities since the Renaissance and in the establishment of a proper papal museum, the Museo Pio-Clementino.

The establishment of the Museo Pio-Clementino shows that the papacy recognized, not so long after Piranesi, that Rome could exploit its position as a tourist centre, in the way that Venice had done. The extension of the papal collection was also in part a by-product of a remarkable expansion of the market for antiquities chiefly due, it seems, to the apparently inexhaustible appetite of English *milordi* such as Lord Lansdowne (fig. 8). As prices rose the temptation to sell was harder for the old, impoverished Roman families to resist. Indeed, it was the English attempt to buy the Maffei collection which prompted Clement XIV to secure it for the Vatican. The appetite of the *milordi* also stimulated extensive and successful speculative excavation in the Campagna from which, in turn, the papacy claimed some of its best pieces for the Pio-Clementino.

Piranesi occupied, towards the end of his life, a prominent place in this busy, but shady, market. He was involved as a speculator in the excavations, as a dealer, as a restorer and, doubtless, as a forger. He was friendly, or had at least an understanding, with such dealer-painters, dealer-sculptors, dealer-*ciceroni* and dealer-bankers as Gavin Hamilton, Cavaceppi, Nollekens, Byres and Jenkins. An idea of the works which passed through his hands may be obtained from his *Vasi, candelabri, cippi*...Among them was one of the finest examples of Roman carving extant, the Warwick Vase, and a number of pieces assembled by Piranesi from miscellaneous antique fragments (Plates 85 and 86). The majority of his customers were English.

Although Piranesi at the outset of his career was most closely associated with the French artistic colony in Rome, the English had always been among the chief patrons of his archaeological enterprises, although, through a series of misunderstandings, Lord Charlemont, to whom Piranesi proposed to dedicate the *Antichità romane* volumes, disappointed the artist (see Plates 46–48). This led Piranesi to an offensive, but partly justified denunciation, disguised as a defence, which gave him a taste for polemical writing. This talent he was able to indulge fully in 1761 in his *Della magnificenza ed architettura de' Romani*, a long attack on the theory, increasingly popular especially in France, that Greek architecture was purer than that of the ancient Romans who had copied and debased it.

Piranesi claimed that Roman architecture derived from the Etruscans and not, in the most important features, from the Greeks; and he followed other Italian theorists in making great claims for the Etruscans as heirs to Egyptian civilization. Piranesi's emphasis on the growth of Roman civilization independent of Greece and his belief in its potential for regrowth, were perhaps derived, as John Wilton-Ely has recently proposed, from the ideas of Giambattista Vico. One can understand how Piranesi, with his enthusiasm for very early Italian engineering achievements such as the Cloaca Maxima or the Emissario of Lake Albano, could claim that these works possessed a more monumental grandeur than did the architecture of Greece, especially since he had no first-hand knowledge of Greek buildings. But he had to shift his ground entirely in order to claim superiority for Roman ornaments: he could not deny their derivation from the Greeks, so instead he claimed that they corrected the faults of the Greeks (Plate 59).

In his arguments Piranesi invoked two sets of standards, those of Vitruvius and those of eighteenth-century rationalist theories which argued that architecture should be elementary and unadorned. His reading of the Venetian theorist Carlo Lodoli, combined with his belief that the basis of architecture must lie in an understanding of stone, led him to ridicule as illogical Greek architectural principles based on the translation of timber structures into marble. But the barbaric splendour of much Roman art which Piranesi so ardently loved and his own bizarre corruptions of Roman ornamentation seen in his *Magnificent Port* (Plate 33) and in the dedicatory plate to the third volume of *Antichità romane* (Plate 47), for example, could not be defended with such rationalist arguments.

In the dedication of the *Campus Martius* Piranesi remarked on how the ancients themselves departed from the 'rules'. Although in his earlier publications Piranesi had condemned this practice, by 1761 he was not certain: perhaps it was decadence, he said, perhaps it was a justifiable desire for novelty. But by 1765, in a dialogue entitled *Parere su l'architettura* appended to a further attack on the French theorists, he completely abandoned all rationalist and all Vitruvian standards, while ingeniously pretending to be simply continuing the arguments of the *Della magnificenza* of 1761. Now at last all his latent personal tendencies towards fantastic invention were frankly indulged, and Piranesi published, in illustration of this thesis, designs for architecture as extravagant and overloaded with ornament as anything ever designed before or since (Plates 68 and 69). During the next few years Piranesi was also at work on schemes for interior decoration, for coaches, for furniture and for chimneypieces which he published in 1769 as *Diverse maniere d'adornare i camini ed ogni altra parte degli edifizi*, with a prefatory defence of Egyptian and Tuscan architecture. Some of his ideas for furnishings are monstrous, a few are elegant, but all, again, are full of bizarre novelties (Plates 79–83). Of those that were carried out and survive, most, and especially the chimneypieces in British houses, are far more attractive and restrained than one might suppose from the prints (Plate 84).

The investigations of the origins of ancient architecture generated, in Piranesi's case, an awareness of the relativity of classical canons. And ironically, as the idea of impersonal archaeological imitation in architecture gained strength, Piranesi, although himself an archaeologist, reacted against such blind repetition in favour of personal originality. Coincidentally, the related demand for 'modernity' in art came in the eighteenth century with the growth of museums and the increasing consciousness of the traditional which they encouraged. Piranesi's case is not an isolated one. A parallel to Piranesi may be detected in the career of the English architect, George Dance the younger, who, when in Rome in the early 1760s, climbed scaffolding to measure the columns of the Temple of Castor and Pollux, known to him as the Temple of Jupiter (Plate 16), and had casts made of their distinctive corinthian capitals. At Tivoli Dance later noted Palladio's errors in describing the Temple of Vesta. In these archaeological beginnings, as was also the case in the late 1750s with Robert Adam, Dance must have been inspired by Piranesi, who was also interested in the capitals of the Temple of Jupiter, which he believed to have been inadequately depicted by Desgodetz. Yet in later years Piranesi seems to have encouraged Dance in most unclassical directions. Dance's Egyptian chimneypiece at Lansdowne House (fig. 8) was perhaps inspired by the *Diverse maniere*; his invention of a novel ionic capital using ammonite fossils instead of the conventional volutes was inspired by an idea tossed out by Piranesi as to the origin of that order; and the ceremonial swords and maces which Dance stuck on the fluted gothic piers of his quasi-oriental Guildhall façade were surely suggested by similar ornaments included by Piranesi in the plates attached to his *Parere su l'architettura* and used by him on the façade of his own Santa Maria del Priorato (Plate 75).

But if Piranesi looked forward to the highly personal peculiarities of Dance's work, he also looked back to the glories of the Italian baroque and he did so with renewed interest at a time when those glories were dismissed by almost all 'men of taste'. Not only were all the compositional principles of Piranesi's etchings derived from the baroque theatre, but his love of witty devices, such as fallen masonry breaking out of the front plane of his designs or his fictive maps and scrolls, was also baroque. His own figures derive from those created by such baroque artists as Salvator Rosa or Magnasco (fig. 6), and in sculpture his taste was for the work of Bernini's successors, such as Legros. In 1772, in a quarrel with the Accademia di San Luca over a monument which its members proposed to erect to Pio Balestra in Santi Martina e Luca, he cited, as an example which they should follow, the shrine of St. Ignatius in the Gesù. The suggestion must have made the Accademia's principal, the hellenist Anton Raphael Mengs, shudder. That was certainly Piranesi's intention.

The period of Piranesi's preoccupation with creating and justifying his self-consciously personal and modern style coincided with the pontificate of the Rezzonico

fig. 9   Thomas de THOMON
Palace and Bridge Seen through an Arch
London, British Museum (Department of
Prints and Drawings). Pen and brown ink
with watercolour 26·9 × 43 cm.

De Thomon, after a long residence in Italy,
returned to France in the mid-1780s only to go
into exile at the time of the Revolution,
eventually settling in Russia as the court
architect of Tsar Alexander I. This drawing,
like Hubert Robert's painting at Dunkerque
(fig. 10), was clearly indebted to Piranesi's *A
Magnificent Bridge* (Plate 4) and his view of the
Arch of Constantine (Plate 15). But at the
same time it is softened by a rococo pastoral
character which is entirely French.

pope, Clement XIII, who, as a Venetian, patronized his
compatriot and provided him, at last, with architectural commissions. At Clement's request Piranesi pre-
pared designs for remodelling the sanctuary of San
Giovanni in Laterano. His ideas were not executed but
the beautiful and detailed drawings which were
presented to the pope's nephew, Cardinal Giovanni
Battista Rezzonico, have recently turned up in the
United States.

In this same period, 1765–67, Piranesi also designed
the complete rebuilding of Santa Maria del Priorato,
the church of the Knights of Malta on the Aventine
together with a small piazza at the entrance to the
knights' adjacent villa. Santa Maria del Priorato is, as
the Lateran sanctuary would have been if built, among
the last few full-blooded baroque buildings of the
eighteenth century (Plates 75–78).

It is chiefly the dramatic effect of the interior of
Santa Maria del Priorato which is baroque: concealed
lighting illuminates and enlarges the apse, against
which the altar and the statue of St. Basil in ecstasy are
silhouetted. The ornament contains many novelties
inspired by the devices of the knights and of the
Rezzonico family, together, of course, with variants on
antique motifs. But this inventiveness is itself of a
distinctly baroque type. In creating capitals which
incorporate the Rezzonico fortress and eagles, Piranesi
was following the example of the seventeenth-century
architects who utilized the emblems of the Barberini or
Chigi families in this way. And in addition to his
variants on antique motifs Piranesi made ample use of
the stylized sunbursts and pancake clouds popularized
by Bernini.

The projects for the sanctuary of San Giovanni in
Laterano (Plates 72–74) are even more clearly baroque,
and in all his schemes for the Lateran, perhaps because
he wished to harmonize his work with the character of
Borromini's nave, Piranesi borrowed ideas from that
architect at a time when every guidebook warned
against Borromini's 'licentious' example. The most
extravagant project involved raising the sanctuary roof
of San Giovanni to obtain clerestory lighting, which
would have been concealed from the nave, for the half-
dome of the apse. And within this illuminated apse
Piranesi wished to erect a free-standing columnar
screen. This idea was anticipated by the Temple of
Vesta design in his *Prima parte*, but the young Piranesi
would never have dared to deny the load-bearing logic

of his pilasters as he did in those Lateran designs, in which the pilasters are hollow cases into which descend vast garlands which begin life coiling round the clerestory windows!

For all his defence of Roman against Greek architecture and in spite of his last-ditch defence of baroque licence against neo-classical strictures, Piranesi's final work was a series of etchings of the ruins of Greek doric temples at Paestum, whose stark and primitive character was then so fervently admired by his hellenist opponents. Piranesi died in 1778, before he had quite completed the work, but the plates and the drawings for them (Plates 88–90) show him fully responsive to the sublime ruins, while the text perhaps only half pretends that they might be 'Italian' in origin. So we are left with another complication in this artist's relationship with the artistic trends of his time.

Surveying Piranesi's career as a whole one can hardly fail to be impressed by his versatility. And for this reason it is very hard to assess his influence in general terms. After his death he continued for a while to be a popular artist; impressions were still taken from his plates which his sons took to Paris and the merits of his *Vedute* could hardly have been fully eclipsed by the pedestrian Roman views made by Luigi Rossini in the

fig. 10 Hubert ROBERT
Port Orné d'Architecture
Dunkerque, Musée de Dunkerque. Oil on
canvas 105 × 145 cm, 1760.

Robert arrived in Rome in 1754 and stayed
there for ten years, resident at the French
Académie and pensioner there from 1759,
working in a manner derived from Panini
whom he knew. On his return to France in
1765 he continued as a prolific painter but was
also involved in the design of gardens and of
interior decoration. On the relatively rare
occasions when Robert was sublime as distinct
from picturesque one may detect the influence
of Piranesi, as in this work, which Mme.
Roland-Michel, in the exhibition catalogue
Piranèse et les Français, has compared with
Piranesi's *A Magnificent Bridge* (Plate 4). The
vault of the main arch is coffered in imitation
of the Basilica of Maxentius, above which is
The Verospi Jove, whilst *The Dioscuri of Monte
Cavallo* stands on the buttresses of the bridge
behind. The figures do nothing to enhance the
awe-inspiring character of the setting.

fig. 11 Charles-Louis CLÉRISSEAU
Capriccio
Leningrad, Hermitage Museum. Pen, brown
ink and gouache 60·5 × 47·2 cm.

Clérisseau was in Rome as a pensioner of the
French Académie from 1749 until 1754 and
was later drawing instructor, draughtsman and
companion of the Adam brothers on their
Italian travels in the 1750s and 1760s. This
gouache from the series owned by Catherine
II, Empress of Russia, shows a famous antique,
the seated *Menander of the Vatican* reversed, in a
fanciful setting. It is exactly the same type of
work as Piranesi's *capriccio* with the tomb of
Marcus Agrippa (Plate 7), but quieter in
mood, the buildings are caressed by the
sunlight and populated by the most amiable
peasantry.

fig. 12 Charles Michel-Ange CHALLE
Interior of a Temple Consecrated to Victory
London, British Museum (Department of
Prints and Drawings). Black chalk, pen, brown
ink and grey wash 46 × 60·7 cm.

Challe was perhaps the French artist who was
most influenced by Piranesi. He must have
had access to Piranesi's drawings as well as to
the etchings when he was in Rome from 1742
to 1749, at first as a pensioner of the French
Académie. He became Professor of Perspective
at the Académie in 1758 and Dessinateur du
Cabinet du Roi in 1764. He was celebrated for
the decorations he provided for the theatre, for
royal *fêtes* and *pompes funèbres*. In these
decorations Piranesi was not forgotten, and
Challe devoted the last years of his life to
translating Piranesi into French.

early 1820s. Nevertheless the fact that Rossini did issue
over a hundred views must indicate that Piranesi was
passing from fashion. At the same date the *Carceri*
etchings gained Piranesi a posthumous reputation as a
romantic visionary, but it is significant that De
Quincey in his famous passage on these etchings
described them as gothic, and it is significant also that
Piranesi's manner was adopted not by etchers of
classical antiquities but by George Cuitt, who needed
dramatic chiaroscuro and rampant vegetation to
conceal his amateur drawing of gothic abbeys in his
etchings of the 1820s. Piranesi's reputation as an
archaeologist vanished very quickly and by the 1830s
Roman archaeology, unlike gothic archaeology, ceased
to be the business of many creative architects.

What Piranesi himself built on the Aventine was
more quickly forgotten than any of his other works.
However, his published decorations in the Egyptian
style (Plates 82 and 83) proved highly influential or at
least prophetic. And it is also arguable that Piranesi's
early ideas for colossal temples, mausolea, triumphal
bridges and ports, which were so quickly taken up by
the French in Rome in the mid-eighteenth century,
were the ancestors of the hundreds of megalomaniacal
projects for temples of war or peace or national glory
which were designed all over Europe at the time of the
Napoleonic wars. Indeed, Piranesi's ideas were also the
ultimate ancestors of Giuseppe Sacconi's Vittorio
Emanuele Monument in Rome, which would so
interest art historians if only it existed as a drawing
attributed to an eighteenth-century architect rather
than as a structure designed in 1884.

individual that he could not have founded a school.
The better artists with whom we know him to have
been closely associated resisted his spell. For instance,
Hubert Robert (fig. 10) and Charles-Louis Clérisseau
(fig. 11) certainly produced some Piranesian views, but
for the most part their work is in quite distinct styles,
and among the French it was the less talented Charles
Michel-Ange Challe who imitated Piranesi most

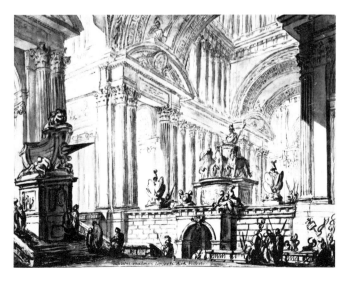

closely (fig. 12). So too did Jean-Laurent LeGeay who had worked with Piranesi etching little views for Fausto Amidei in the 1740s. LeGeay's etchings of vases, fountains and tombs look like parodies of Piranesi's earliest manner by an artist without any understanding of Piranesi's baroque compositions, but with an original dash of grotesque fantasy (fig. 13) which anticipates Walt Disney. These etchings were certainly executed long before their date of publication but it is impossible to believe that they influenced Piranesi, as some scholars have suggested, and there is no firm evidence that they are early enough in date to have done so.

The younger Dance has already been mentioned as one of Piranesi's English friends, but although he assimilated a few of Piranesi's ideas it could never be said that he worked in Piranesi's manner. Robert Adam knew Piranesi in the 1750s, almost certainly through Clérisseau, and at the end of his Roman stay he produced drawings which suggest that Piranesi had made a more profound impression upon his imagination than is in fact suggested by the architecture which he erected upon his return to Britain. Although Damie Stillman has shown how Adam took up hints from the *Diverse maniere* for his Etruscan rooms and his chimney-pieces of the 1770s, neither the characteristic delicacy and grace of Adam's interior decorations, nor indeed the cosmetic thinness of his less successful façades, can be considered typical of Piranesi. Other English architects whom Piranesi knew, Robert Mylne and Thomas Harrison, for instance, remained similarly independent.

Nevertheless, it is in England, in the domestic museum established by Dance's pupil and Adam's admirer, Sir John Soane, that we may most clearly detect the survival of Piranesi's spirit. In some rooms of Soane's museum there are a few relics of ancient civilizations, inserted as quotations in the poetry of Soane's own architecture, itself quite as novel and as erudite as Piranesi's; but elsewhere mysterious top-lit chambers are encrusted with fragments of architecture, statues, busts and urns, and original marble is perplexingly mingled with casts (fig. 14). The eye has no rest amidst all this picturesque diversity and bizarre incongruity. This is not the place for those who go to art hoping that it will compose the mind. And the prints of Piranesi are no more conducive to mental calm. Among the many great artists who have portrayed the ruins of antiquity Piranesi is surely alone in never showing human beings at rest in their shade.

fig. 13 Jean-Laurent LEGEAY
Rovine: title-page
Etching 19·2 × 16·4 cm. 1768.

LeGeay was resident in Paris from 1737 until early in 1742 and it has been supposed that it was in those years that he produced the series of designs for vases, fountains, tombs and ruins (*rovine*) which were published in 1767 and 1768. In this way works such as this title-page have been proposed as crucial influences on Piranesi rather than as what they appear to have been, curious, personal interpretations of one or two themes in Piranesi's *Opere varie*.

fig. 14 Joseph Michael GANDY
The Dome of Sir John Soane's Museum in 1813
London, Sir John Soane's Museum.
Watercolour 125·7 × 71·1 cm. 1813.

Sir John Soane's Museum seems even more Piranesian than in fact it is in drawings such as this by Soane's draughtsman, Gandy. It is appropriate that this museum contains many of Piranesi's drawings of Paestum and a number of architectural fragments which came from the collection of Henry Holland, formed originally in Rome by C. H. Tatham and Richard Westmacott in the 1790s and including pieces previously in Piranesi's collection.

Select Bibliography

G. L. Bianconi, 'Elogio Storico del Cavaliere Giambattista Piranesi celebre antiquario ed incisore di Roma', *Antologia Romana*, vols. XXXIV–XXXVI (Rome, 1779).

J. C. Legrand, *Notice historique sur la vie et les oeuvres de J.-B. Piranesi* (MS in the Bibliothèque Nationale, Paris; published in *Nouvelles de l'Estampe*, vol. V, 1969 and in Morazzoni, q.v.).

H. Focillon, *Giovanni-Battista Piranesi (1720–1778)*. Paris, 1918.

G. Morazzoni, *G. B. Piranesi, Notizie biographiche*. Milan, 1921.

A. M. Hind, *Giovanni Battista Piranesi. A Critical Study of His Published Works and Detailed Catalogue of the Prisons and the Views of Rome*. London, 1922.

F. Stampfle, 'An Unknown Group of Drawings by G. B. Piranesi', *Art Bulletin*, vol. XXX (1948).

F. Stampfle, *Giovanni Battista Piranesi, an Exhibition of Drawings* (catalogue of exhibition at Pierpont Morgan Library, New York). New York, 1949.

A. H. Mayor, *Giovanni Battista Piranesi*. New York, 1952.

H. Thomas, *The Drawings of Giovanni Battista Piranesi*. London, 1954.

J. Fleming, *Robert Adam and his Circle in Edinburgh and Rome*. London, 1962.

J. Harris, 'Le Geay, Piranesi and International Neo-Classicism in Rome 1740–1750' *and* D. Stillman, 'Robert Adam and Piranesi', *Essays in the History of Architecture Presented to Rudolf Wittkower* (D. Fraser, H. Hibbard and M. Lewine, eds.). London, 1967.

S. Gavuzzo Stewart, 'Nota sulle Carceri piranesiane', *L'Arte* (1971).

J. Wilton-Ely (ed.), *G. B. Piranesi: the Polemical Works*. New York, 1972.

D. Nyberg et al, *Giovanni Battista Piranesi: Drawings and Etchings at Columbia University, New York* (catalogue of exhibition at Low Memorial Library, Columbia University, New York). New York, 1972.

R. Bacou, *Piranèse, gravures et dessins*. Paris, 1974 (English translation: London, 1975).

A. Rowan, 'Wedderburn Castle', *Country Life*, vol. CLVI (8 August 1974).

J. Scott, *Piranesi*. London, 1975.

R. Wittkower, *Studies in the Italian Baroque*. London, 1975.

G. Brunel et al, *Piranèse et les Français 1740–1790* (catalogue of exhibition at Villa Medici, Rome; Palais des Etats de Bourgogne, Dijon; and Hôtel de Sully, Paris). Rome, 1976.

Mention must also be made of an important contribution by J. Wilton-Ely, *The Mind and Art of Giovanni Battista Piranesi* (London, 1978), which was published after the present book went to press.

1   *Two Colonnaded Courtyards*

LONDON, British Museum (Department of Prints and Drawings). Pen and brown ink with a light wash, over a sketch in black chalk clearly visible in the sky 14·1 × 21 cm. c.1740.

Perhaps only the crowning statues suggest the artist's later drawing style. The trophies suspended between the applied columns of the piers are, for Piranesi, remarkably discrete. The columns here, as is not uncommon in the *Prima parte* etchings, are unfluted, but after the early 1740s the clean unbroken surface of an unfluted shaft was something Piranesi etched only once or twice.

Gruppo di Scale ornato di magnifica Architettura, le quali stanno disposte in modo che conducano a vary piani, e specialmente ad una Rotonda che serve per rappresentanze teatrali.

2 *Prima parte*, as revised in *Opere varie* of 1750, plate eleven: *a Suite of Stairways*
Etching 25 × 37 cm. c.1743.

This was the eighth plate in the first edition of *Prima parte* of 1743 where it was entitled simply 'Loco Magnifico d'Architettura'. It is nothing but a splendid perspective and as such resembles the early drawing in the British Museum of the two courtyards (Plate 1). Along with all but one of the plates of *Prima parte*, this etching was included in Piranesi's *Opere varie*.

(*opposite*)
3 *Prima parte*, as revised in *Opere varie* of 1750, plate fifteen [but not numbered]:
Ancient Temple of Vesta
Etching 34·5 × 25 cm. c.1743.

This was plate ten in the first edition of *Prima parte* of 1743. The temple was inspired by the Pantheon, the large vase on the left by *The Borghese Vase*, the tempietto perhaps by the Temple of Vesta by the Tiber, and among the statues there is one derived from *The Farnese Hercules*, which also appears in the frontispiece to the 1748 *Vedute di Roma* (Plate 17). No comparable domed interior was actually erected in eighteenth-century Europe, with the exception of James Wyatt's Pantheon of 1770–72, a building in Oxford Street consecrated to the pleasures of London society.

Tempio antico inventato e disegnato alla maniera di quelli che si fabbricavano in onore della Dea Vesta: quindi vedesi in mezzo la grand'Ara, sopra della quale conservavasi dalle Vergini Vestali l'inestinguibile fuoco sacro. Tutta l'opera è Corintia ornata di statue e di bassi rilievi, e di altri ornamenti ancora. Il piano di questo Tempio è notabilmente elevato dal suolo: vedesi in mezzo la Cella rotonda, come lo è pure tutto il gran Vaso del Tempio stesso: quattro loggie portavano ad essa, e per altrettante scale vi si ascendeva. Le parieti del gran Tempio hanno due ordini, sopra il secondo s'incurva una vasta Cupola con isfondati, e rosoni, e termina in una grande apertura, dalla q.te dipende il lume alla Cella che le sta sotto.

Gio Batta Piranesi Arch.° inv, ed incise in Roma l'Anno 1743

Ponte magnifica con Logge, ed Archi eretto da un Imperatore Romano, nel mezzo si vede la Statua Equestre del medesimo. Questo ponte viene veduto ... di un arco d'un lato del Ponte che si unisce al sudetto, come si vede pure nel fondo un medesimo arco attaccato al principal Ponte

4 *Prima parte*, as revised in *Opere varie* of 1750, plate eight: *a Magnificent Bridge*
Etching 24 × 36 cm. c.1743.

The text added when this plate was reissued as part of the *Opere varie* explains that the central opening in the arcade enshrines an equestrian statue, but does not specify the purpose of the smaller bridges attached to the main one. *A Magnificent Bridge* is certainly one of the most powerful in the series and had a great influence both on painters (figs. 9 and 10) and on architects (Plate 70). It is tempting to suppose that the popularity of the idea of the triumphal bridge as a monument celebrating the British victories in the Napoleonic wars reflected the impact of this print.

(*opposite*)
5 *Prima parte*, as revised in *Opere varie* of 1750, plate two: *Carcere Oscura*
Etching 36 × 24 cm. c.1743.

This subject, which is unlike any of the others in *Prima parte*, looks forward to the *Carceri* (Plates 35–42) and back to a tradition of stage designs for dungeons by the Bibiena family and their followers. The text refers to the 'antenna' for torture. This must be the hanging cage in which a prisoner could be suspended and which features in many of the *Carceri* plates.

Gio. Batta. Piranesi Arch.o inven ed incise in Roma

Carcere oscura con Antenna pel suplizio dè malfatori. Sonvi da lungi le Scale, che
conducono al piano e vi si vedono pure all' intorno altre chiuse carceri.

Ruine di Sepolcro antico posto dinanzi ad altre ruine d'un Acquedotto pure antico; sopra gli archi del medesimo v'è il canale, per cui si conduceva l'acqua in Roma.
Gio: Batta Piranesi Architetto inventò, ed incise in Roma. 6

Vestiggi d'antichi Edificj fra i quali evvi l'Urna Sepolcrale tutta d'un pezzo di porfido di Marco Agrippa che oggi serve per il Sepolcro di Clemente XII. Si vede anche un pezzo di Guglia con caratteri Egizj, ed in lontano un Vestibolo di antico Tempio rovinato.
Gio: Batta Piranesi Architetto inventò, ed incise di Roma.

(above left)
6   *Prima parte*, as revised in *Opere varie* of 1750, plate six: *Ruins of a Tomb*
Etching 36·4 × 24·6 cm. c.1743.

A very similar etching, but of a different size, served as the third plate in the first edition of *Prima parte* of 1743. This new plate is not likely to have been made as late as 1750, by which date Piranesi's revisions would have been more extensive. The fragment of a frieze and the upturned corinthian capital were probably inspired by Piranesi's studies of the Temple of Vespasian. The distant aqueduct looks forward to Piranesi's later fascination with Roman engineering. In the signature the young artist was eager to stress that he was both an architect and a Roman resident.

(above right)
7   *Prima parte*, as revised in *Opere varie* of 1750, plate five: *Remains of Ancient Buildings*
Etching 33·6 × 25·5 cm. c.1743.

This plate was not included in the first edition of *Prima parte* of 1743 and is therefore probably later, although perhaps only a little later, in date. The 'furry' and stippled strokes, also the forms of the festooned creepers and foreground reeds, are very close to those in a small view of the Baths of Titus, one of the earliest of the little *Vedute* of the 1740s. *Remains of Ancient Buildings* is more dramatic than *Ruins of a Tomb* (Plate 6) and less reminiscent of the ruin pieces etched by Marco Ricci. Although Piranesi carefully recorded the wave-pattern on the edge of the sarcophagus lid and the egg and dart moulding on the half-sunk entablature in the lower left foreground, these are hardly visible and reveal the young artist's imperfect control of etching. The sphinx and the Egyptian characters on the fragment of an obelisk behind the column base look forward to Piranesi's later interest in Egyptian ornament. The chief item here, the sarcophagus or 'bath' of Marcus Agrippa, is also connected with Egypt, for it was fashioned from a single block of porphyry. For a long time this celebrated sarcophagus was to be seen in the portico of the Pantheon, but by the time Piranesi came to Rome it had been appropriated for the tomb of Clement XII in the Capella Corsini in San Giovanni in Laterano. Piranesi etched it again for the dedication page of his *Campus Martius* of 1762. The recipient of that dedication was Robert Adam and, as David Udy has pointed out, the etching surely inspired Adam's 1768 design for the Shelburne House stool, now in the mausoleum at Bowood, a precocious example of neo-classical furniture. Reduced replicas of the sarcophagus in *giallo antico* or some other ancient marble were popular chimneypiece ornaments of the late eighteenth and early nineteenth centuries.

8   *Preparatory Drawing for an Ancient Imperial Mausoleum*
EDINBURGH, National Gallery of Scotland (Department of Prints and Drawings). Pen, brown ink, with grey wash, over a sketch in black chalk, with the main lines incised 34·7 × 24·3 cm. c.1743.

This is a careful and detailed study in reverse for the etching of an ancient mausoleum, clearly executed at the time of the *Prima parte*, probably for the *Seconda parte*, but not published until 1750 in *Opere varie* as the third plate. The incised lines would seem to indicate that it was transferred on to the copper plate, but in the etching there are a number of differences. The attic above the pediment, which was changed to a segmental design, is shown in ruin and instead of poplars there is a higher register to the building. The strange invention of fluted cones with spiral bands rising out of complex sarcophagi foreshadows the more robust perversities of the *Magnificent Port* (Plate 33).

(*above left*)
9   *Sketch for a Frontispiece*
LONDON, British Museum (Department of Prints and Drawings). Pen and brown ink with wash over a slight black chalk sketch 27·8 × 19·6 cm. c.1745.

This drawing has been plausibly connected with the skeletons in Piranesi's Tiepolo-esque *Grotteschi* (Plates 12 and 13). The drawing style here is in fact slightly reminiscent of Tiepolo's in character, although frenetic rather than fluent. The suggestion that this is a design for a frontispiece can only be tentative. It could represent an idea for, or from, a painting or a tomb or a catafalque. However, even if it had been carved by Piranesi's friend, the sculptor Corradini, these skeletons would have had to have been shrouded if the marble was to have held together.

(*above right*)
10   *Festival Gondola* or *Bissona*
NEW YORK, Pierpont Morgan Library (bequest of Junius S. Morgan and gift of Henry S. Morgan). Pen and brown ink wash over black chalk 29·6 × 68·3 cm. c.1745.

On the verso are drawings for rococo ornament and for picture frames. This drawing would seem to have been executed during Piranesi's brief return to Venice in 1744–45. Ornamental gondolas of this type may be seen in several of Canaletto's paintings of festivals on the Grand Canal. Piranesi's interest in the decorative arts, so apparent in this period, was to revive in the 1760s.

(*opposite bottom*)
11   *Spectacular Theatrical Performance*
PARIS, La Société des Architectes Diplômés par le Gouvernement. Brown ink and wash over red chalk 51·2 × 76·5 cm. c.1745.

Although Piranesi was constantly indebted in his compositions to ideas which have a scenographic origin, this drawing is his only known work which actually represents a theatrical performance. Angels greet an ascending figure in the centre. To the right and left a seething chorus blasts trumpets and waves arms. The rich console brackets of the proscenium arch, if such it be, recall some mannerisms of the Bibiena family's designs of this sort. The festooned medallions also appear in the *Grotteschi*. Some of the 'machinery' may be for fireworks, and this sheet may be the *feu d'artifice* drawn by Piranesi and presented by him in 1746 to the French sculptor Jacques Saly to celebrate the latter's recovery from a dangerous illness. Such a drawing is mentioned in the sale of Saly's effects in 1776.

12　*Opere varie*: *Fantastic Landscape with a Herm*
Etching 39·5 × 55 cm. c.1745.

Many of the details in this etching, the antique reliefs and the herm, the halberds, trumpets, snakes and bones, the male nude seen from the back, the pine tree and the palm, appear in Tiepolo's *Scherzi* etchings (fig. 3), which Piranesi must have seen on his visit to Venice in the mid-1740s. *Fantastic Landscape with a Herm* is one of the unnumbered plates of the *Grotteschi* published in *Opere varie* (1750).

13 *Opere varie: Fantastic Landscape with a Stranded Dolphin*
Etching 39 × 54·5 cm. c.1745.

In the lower right-hand corner we see a palette and brushes and elsewhere medals and fragments of
architecture and sculpture. The emblems of the arts often appeared in allegories of the vanity of
worldly glory, but there is surely no simple explanation for their presence in this etching, another
of the unnumbered plates of the *Grotteschi* published in *Opere varie* of 1750. Rococo scrolls are
animated into snakes and the dolphin, that creature much favoured by rococo artists, is stranded in
the upper right-hand corner. The distant cypresses were not a type of tree depicted frequently by
Piranesi, but they do appear in the background of the *Remains of Ancient Buildings* (Plate 7), the
connection to which is reinforced by the prominence of the antique sarcophagus in this etching.

Arco di Settimio Severo, e Caracalla nel Foro Boario appresso S. Giorgio in Velabro

Piranesi f.

Tom. I.

PIRANESI F.   ARCO DI COSTANTINO IN ROMA

Piranesi fecit. Vestigj del Tempio di Giove Statore. 1. Tempio d'Antonino e Faustina. 2. Tempio della Pace. Tav.

16 *Archi trionfali*, originally *Antichità romane de' tempi della republica e de' primi imperatori*, plate ten: *the Forum with the Columns of the Temple of Castor and Pollux*
Etching 12·5 × 26·5 cm. 1748.

These three columns were part of the continuous screen around the shrine of the temple of the twin gods. Although this was the earliest and most sacred building in the Forum, it was rebuilt several times in antiquity. The columns may date from the restorations carried out under Augustus by his heir Tiberius, but they could also date from the end of the first century A.D. Piranesi, together with most antiquarians of the eighteenth century, believed the columns to have belonged to a Temple of Jupiter. The capitals have distinctively intertwined spirals rising above the acanthus leaves of the corinthian order. A cast was made of one of these capitals by Dance in 1763, fifteen years after Piranesi's etching, and Piranesi himself illustrated the Castor and Pollux spirals in the seventh plate of *Della magnificenza*. It is interesting that Piranesi permitted the landscape to break through into the title of the present print, a device which he did not employ in the earliest of his big *Vedute di Roma*.

(*opposite top*)
14 *Varie vedute di Roma antica e moderna*: *the Arch of Septimus Severus*
Etching 13 × 19 cm. c.1746.

The majority of Piranesi's small views of Rome may be dated to the period 1745–48, although a few may have been executed earlier. The plates from Piranesi's *Varie vedute* were still being used for other guidebooks twenty years later, and the version of his *Arch of Septimus Severus* illustrated here comes from the leading guide of the 1760s, Ridolfino Venuti's *Accurata e succinta descrizione topographica delle antichità di Roma*, published in two volumes in 1763. The page reference in this case was partially scratched out because it no longer corresponded with the guide it was meant to illustrate. The Arch of Septimus Severus usually refers to the imposing triumphal arch which is so prominent a feature in Piranesi's view of the Campo Vaccino (Plate 18), but this arch is the one generally called the Arco degli Argentari, erected by the money-changers in honour of Septimus Severus and his family in the Forum Boarium, the oldest Roman market.

(*opposite bottom*)
15 *Archi trionfali*, originally *Antichità romane de' tempi della republica e de' primi imperatori*, plate nine: *the Arch of Constantine*
Etching 13 × 26 cm. 1748.

In both shape and size the *Archi trionfali* etchings are very close to Vasi's etchings of Rome, also published in the late 1740s. The use of the foreground arch as a frame was much favoured by Piranesi's compatriot Canaletto, nowhere more brilliantly than in his etching *The Portico with a Lantern*. Piranesi had used the device earlier in his own design for *A Magnificent Bridge* (Plate 4) in the *Prima parte*. The Arch of Constantine, erected in A.D. 315 to celebrate the Emperor Constantine's victory over Maxentius, was the most prominent of the four surviving triumphal arches of Rome, but it was chiefly valued because it incorporated relief sculpture from earlier monuments of the Trajanic, Hadrianic and Aurelian periods.

17 *Vedute di Roma*, frontispiece
Etching 48·5 × 63 cm. c.1748.

By masking the copper plate, Piranesi published this frontispiece as two separate pieces of the *Opere varie*. The palm, the smoke, the spatial confusion, the piling up of fragments, the medallion portraits and the foreground vegetation all suggest that this design may have originated as one of the *Grotteschi*. *The Farnese Hercules* appears on the left, seen from behind, and the central figure is the porphyry torso of *Pallas*, restored as *Roma*, to be seen in a niche behind the statue of Marcus Aurelius on the Capitol. But the figure is studied from an odd angle, the pose is reversed, and Piranesi re-broke one of the added white marble arms and made the remaining figure appear as of a single-coloured material.

Veduta di Campo Vaccino

18   *Vedute di Roma: the Campo Vaccino*
Etching 38 × 54·5 cm. c.1748.

The 'Campo Vaccino' was the eighteenth-century name for the Forum, which was then used for grazing cattle; no cattle were included in this etching but they do appear in *The Forum with the Columns of the Temple of Castor and Pollux* (Plate 16). The viewpoint is high so that the artist can include as many monuments as possible, but also because we are meant to imagine ourselves on the high ground of the Capitol. The excavations, which completely transformed the view as depicted by Piranesi, began in the early nineteenth century, but when Turner painted this scene it had still retained its pastoral character and cattle continued to graze there in 1880 before Lanciani's excavations.

(*overleaf*)
19   *Vedute di Roma: St. Peter's from the Piazza*
Etching 38 × 54 cm. c.1748.

This is one of the earliest of the *Vedute di Roma* and the highly decorated coach approaching the trough from the left recalls Piranesi's design for a gondola (Plate 10). Against the back of the trough a beggar urinates, torrentially.

1. Palazzo Pontificio fabbricato da Sisto V.
2. Logge di Giulio II architettura di Bramante Lazzari, e
dipinte da Raffaelle D'Urbino.

Veduta della Basilica e G

za di S. Pietro in Vaticano

Veduta della Piazza di Monte Cavallo

20 *Vedute di Roma*: the Piazza di Monte Cavallo
Etching 36·5 × 54 cm. c.1748.

One of the seven hills of Rome, the Quirinal, vulgarly called 'Monte Cavallo' on account of the colossal antique horses erected there, achieved a novel importance in 1574 when the Buoncompagni pope, Gregory XIII, erected a palace, seen to the right of Piranesi's etching, as a papal summer residence. The architect for this undertaking was Mascarino. The Quirinal Palace soon replaced the Vatican as the pope's chief residence and today it is the presidential palace of the Republic of Italy. To the left of Piranesi's view we see the papal barracks and military parades are still a common spectacle here. This etching represents the only notable occasion on which Piranesi placed the sun in his sky. In the first state of *The Piazza di Monte Cavallo* there is no lettering on the base of the colossal statues identifying them as the work of the Greek sculptors Phidias and Praxiteles, but the legend makes it clear that Piranesi accepted these attributions, as did many scholars even seventy years later. In the debate over what subject was represented Piranesi favoured the idea of Alexander and Bucephalus.

(*opposite top*)
21 *Vedute di Roma*: the Piazza della Rotonda
Etching 39 × 54·5 cm. c.1748.

Although the general impression of the scale of Rome is much more reliable in Piranesi's earlier *Vedute* than in the later ones, his 'wide-angle' perspective here gives one a misleading impression of the size of this piazza.

(*opposite bottom*)
22 *Vedute di Roma*: the Pantheon
Etching 46·5 × 68·5 cm. 1761 [according to Francesco Piranesi's catalogue].

Whereas Piranesi earlier depicted the Pantheon as part of the Piazza della Rotonda (Plate 21), he permitted it to dominate this print. A similar change of emphasis occurred when Piranesi treated the Capitol for the second time in the *Vedute* (Plates 28 and 29). The Pantheon was begun and perhaps designed by the Emperor Hadrian in A.D. 118–119, but it replaced another temple also dedicated to all the gods which had been erected by Agrippa, and Hadrian credited his building to Agrippa in the inscription still to be seen on the portico frieze. For this reason, in Piranesi's time and for long afterwards, the building was called Agrippa's Pantheon. The temple was completed by Antoninus Pius and restored by Septimus Severus. The towers flanking the portico were added in the seventeenth century, but have since been removed. They were belfries appropriate to the Pantheon's function as the Christian Church of Santa Maria de' Martiri, also called 'Santa Maria della Rotonda'. Of all the ancient buildings in Rome the Pantheon was the best preserved and most admired.

Veduta della Piazza della Rotonda

Veduta del Pantheon d'Agrippa
oggi Chiesa di S. Maria ad Martyres

Veduta di Piazza Navona

...a le rovine del Circo Agonale

S. Giacomo de Spagnoli,
Fontana Architettata di Michelangelo

Questo fù fabricato da Au
1. Palazzo Orsini ristaura

24   *Vedute di Roma: the Piazza Navona, with Sant' Agnese on the Left*
Etching 46·7 × 55·6 cm. 1773 [according to Francesco Piranesi's catalogue].

It would be hard not to find this late work more exciting than the early view of the Piazza Navona
(Plate 23), but the busy figures and statuary in the foreground of the second version distract from
the architecture and the transition from foreground to middleground, often uncertain in the *Vedute*,
as in, for instance, the view of St. Peter's (Plate 19), is also an embarrassment here. The
characteristically deeply bitten shading of the later etchings is not fully under control on the right-
hand side, where the ink broke through the ridges, possibly because the copper plate was left in the
acid too long.

25   *Vedute di Roma: the Theatre of Marcellus*
Etching 38 × 55 cm. c.1751.

The Theatre of Marcellus, projected by Julius Caesar, was completed by Augustus and dedicated to
Marcellus, his nephew and son-in-law, in about 13 B.C. It could accommodate approximately
20,000 spectators. In Piranesi's print we see the theatre as it is today, with the ground level risen
around it. The ancient remains still seem strangely incorporated into the Palazzo Orsini, but one
side of the theatre was stripped of all accretions as part of the archaeological programme carried
out under Mussolini.

(*preceding page*)
23   *Vedute di Roma: the Piazza Navona, with Sant' Agnese on the Right*
Etching 38·5 × 54·5 cm. c. 1748.

The Piazza Navona is one of the great monuments of baroque urban planning, closely associated
with the pontificate (1644–55) of the Pamphili pope, Innocent X, whose family residence, the
Palazzo Pamphili, designed by the aged Girolamo Rainaldi and executed in the late 1640s with the
assistance of Borromini, stands in the centre of this etching to the left of Sant' Agnese. The Church
of Sant' Agnese, another Pamphili commission, was begun in 1652 by Girolamo Rainaldi and his
son Carlo but was not consecrated until 1672 with an influential concave façade designed by
Borromini. Opposite this façade and dominating the centre of the piazza is Bernini's celebrated
Fountain of Four Rivers, unveiled in 1651 and incorporating personifications of four rivers, the
Danube, the Nile, the Ganges and the Plate, symbols of the four continents, which in turn provide
the foundation for an antique Egyptian obelisk, reconstructed from fragments discovered in the
Circus of Maxentius, not far from the Mausoleum of Cecilia Metella (Plate 53), on the Via Appia.
Across the piazza from the Church of Sant' Agnese is the quattrocento Church of San Giacomo
degli Spagnuoli, begun during the 1455–58 pontificate of the first Borgia pope, Calixtus III, and
including a contribution from Antonio da Sangallo the younger. Piranesi's inclusion of a group of
chair-makers at work in the left foreground is a piece of local colour typical of the early but not of
the late *Vedute*.

licato a Marcello suo Ripote.
assare da Siena Architetto.

TEATRO DI MARCELLO.

2. Cupola di S. Maria in Campitelli.

Piranesi Architetto

Veduta della Basilica di S. Giovanni Laterano

26   *Vedute di Roma*: San Giovanni in Laterano
Etching 37 × 54 cm. c.1748.

This early work shows San Giovanni in Laterano, one of Rome's most venerable churches after St.
Peter's, as it appeared after it was re-dressed in 1736 with a new façade designed by Alessandro
Gallilei. We also see the dome of Gallilei's Capella Corsini, the chapel containing the sarcophagus
of Marcus Agrippa which Piranesi, in his etching of *Remains of Ancient Buildings* (Plate 7) for the
Opere varie, transposed to a semi-rural setting. The majority of the early *Vedute* are devoted to
modern Rome and the series may at first have been conceived of as complementing the *Archi
trionfali* series, which depicted ancient ruins. Three of the four figures positioned on the rampart,
cutting diagonally across the foreground of this etching, recall those in the *Grotteschi* (Plate 12).

(*opposite top*)
27   *Vedute di Roma*: San Giovanni in Laterano
Etching 48 × 69·5 cm. 1775 [according to Francesco Piranesi's catalogue].

This very late example of Piranesi's *Vedute* contrasts strikingly with the early view of the same
façade taken from another angle (Plate 26). In this etching the building looms up before us and the
lighting is far more dramatic, but the composition is less carefully calculated. In the earlier plate
the figures on the ramparts provide a perfect foil to the buildings in the middleground, while the
figures around the inscription in the 1775 version, clumsily drawn and occupying inexplicably
raised ground, play no such active rôle. In the early etching the coach on the right has a decisive
part in balancing the composition, but none of the carriages or huts dotted around on the left of
the later view would be much missed if erased.

(*opposite bottom*)
28   *Vedute di Roma*: the Capitol and the Steps of Santa Maria in Aracoeli
Etching 38 × 53·5 cm. c.1748.

The Capitol, or 'Campidoglio' as it is called by twentieth-century Romans, was the site of the
oldest and most sacred of Roman shrines, the Temple of Jupiter, the heart of Rome and of the
Roman empire, and so, to all educated Europeans of Piranesi's time, saturated with more historical
associations than any other spot in the civilized world. The present piazza was designed by
Michelangelo around the equestrian statue of Marcus Aurelius, and he also designed the ramp
which leads up to it. The steps up to Santa Maria in Aracoeli were constructed in 1348. As with
the subjects of most of Piranesi's earliest *Vedute*, the ramp leading to the Capitol was an obvious
choice, treated from the most obvious and informative viewpoint. This etching stands in contrast to
Piranesi's later and more dramatic view of the Capitol from the side (Plate 29). The canine
encounters on the lower part of the ramp and in the lower left-hand corner are humorous elements
similarly characteristic of the early *Vedute*, as is the broken, fluted column in the lower right-hand
corner, also found in the *Grotteschi* (Plates 12, 13 and 17).

Veduta del Romano Campidoglio con Scalinata che va alla Chiesa d'Araceli

47

29   *Vedute di Roma: the Capitol Seen from the Side of the Central Steps*
Etching 40 × 69 cm. c.1760.

This print is dated to 1775 in Francesco Piranesi's catalogue of his father's work, but this date is, as Hind pointed out, clearly a mistake since the etching was not signed 'Cavaliere', as was all Piranesi's work after his award of a papal knighthood in 1766. Hind, however, wanted to date this plate to as early as 1757 and to link it to the earlier view of the same subject (Plate 28). In fact the earlier and more orthodox view dates from yet earlier than 1757, while this overpowering image is rather later. The dimensions of the plate are typical of the *Vedute* of the 1760s, as is the signature 'Piranesi F.' and the device of incorporating the inscription. The Trophies of Marius, originally designed to fill niches, are, when seen from this angle, endowed with brutal power but divested of any claims to elegance. Piranesi was unable to resist giving the crowning statues of Michelangelo's Palazzo de' Conservatori in the background more animated silhouettes than they possessed at that date.

(*opposite top*)
30   *Vedute di Roma: the Fontana dell' Acqua Giulia*
Etching 38 × 60·5 cm. c.1753.

'Acqua Giulia' is the name of one of the systems of aqueducts which supplied ancient Rome with water. This structure, once a fountain, can still be seen in the Piazza Vittorio Emanuele. Piranesi at first entitled this view *Il Castel dell' Acqua Marcia*, but changed the title after he had made his own archaeological investigations. The Fontana dell' Acqua Giulia was the original site of the so-called Trophies of Marius, set up on the Capitol (Plate 29) in the sixteenth century and believed by Piranesi to have been the Trophies of Octavian. The inclusion of the clothes-line as genre detail is, again, characteristic of the earlier *Vedute*.

(*opposite bottom*)
31   *Vedute di Roma: the Villa Albani*
Etching 43 × 69 cm. 1769.

Building of the Villa Albani, today the Villa Torlonia, on the Via Salaria, was started in 1746 and completed in about 1763. It was the last great Roman residence in the tradition of the villas of the Borghese and Medici families and was the property of Cardinal Alessandro Albani, the *nipote* of Clement XI. Cardinal Albani was the greatest private Roman collector of antiquities of the eighteenth century and the patron of Winckelmann and Mengs as well as the protector of Piranesi. He took an active part in the design of this villa and its gardens, bullying his architect Carlo Marchionni. As with Piranesi's other late *Vedute*, such as that of San Giovanni in Laterano (Plate 27), the foreground is awkwardly composed and, in this case, seems tilted. Piranesi's later view of the Villa Pamphili presents similar problems.

IL CASTEL DELL'ACQUA MARCIA

Veduta della Villa dell'Em.o Sig.r Card.
Alessandro Albani fuori di Porta Salaria

32   *Vedute di Roma: the Golden House of Nero*
Etching 48·5 × 70·5 cm. 1774 [according to Francesco Piranesi's catalogue].

Piranesi believed this building was a part of the Domus Aurea or Golden House of Nero, although most of his contemporaries held that it was Vespasian's Temple of Peace. It is now known that it was the Basilica of Maxentius, begun by that emperor in A.D. 306–312 and completed by his successor, Constantine. It was the last great Roman basilica to have been built. Whatever reservations one might have about some of Piranesi's late *Vedute*, this plate is of the highest quality, and if it 'distorts' it does so only in order to convey what are essential properties of this ruin. The ground was higher in the eighteenth century than it is today, and one can see how Hubert Robert was inspired to paint the vault as if it sprung from the ground itself (fig. 10).

33   *Opere varie: Magnificent Port*
Etching 40 × 55 cm. c.1750.

Although early eighteenth-century architects and scenographers such as Juvarra had sketched the forums and ports of the Romans, no one before Piranesi, except perhaps Mantegna in the fifteenth century, had re-created with comparable conviction the 'wild enormities of ancient magnanimity'. This plate makes an interesting contrast with the earlier *Ancient Temple of Vesta* etching (Plate 3) from *Prima parte*. The idea of buildings enveloping other buildings is common to both, but the ornament here is much more inventive. The river god on the principal arch was modelled on the colossal *Tiber*, then in the Belvedere in the Vatican, but now in the Musée du Louvre, Paris. The urns in their niches to the left and the obelisk to the right recall the design for an ancient mausoleum in *Prima parte*. The lions' heads grip rings on the left-hand side of the arch and spew water on the right-hand side. Wriggling dolphins are contained by the central pediment but tumble out of the right-hand one. The *Opere varie* was published in 1750.

34   *Opere varie*: *Ancient Baths*
Etching 14 × 20 cm. c.1760.

Ancient Baths is one of the supplementary plates added to the *Opere varie* set when it was republished, probably in the early 1760s. The use of the powerful 'primitive' Greek doric order, so alarming to conventional classical taste of the time, was astonishingly precocious. Its first recorded revival since antiquity in European architecture came only a little earlier than Piranesi's etching, with Stuart's temple at Hagley of 1758, and it was not revived in France before the 1770s, nor in Germany before the 1790s. The combination of Greek doric with an arch breaking into the pediment, a very unarchaeological idea, anticipated a favourite theme in Ledoux's architecture. The cumbersome superstructure, however, was not something anyone was likely to imitate in a building which was actually meant to be constructed.

(above left)
35 *Invenzioni capric di carceri*, title-page
Etching 54 × 41·4 cm. c.1745–50.

The fourteen unnumbered plates of the first edition of Piranesi's *Carceri* were dated to 1750 by Francesco Piranesi, but they may well have been executed as early as 1745 when Piranesi returned from Venice. The chained man here is similar in conception to the figures in one of the *Grotteschi* (Plate 12), prints which were certainly Venetian in inspiration, and there is a still earlier state of this title plate in which 'Bouchard', the name of the publisher, is spelt 'Buzard', as a Venetian would have pronounced it. In reworking the *Carceri* plates Piranesi generally retained all the original spontaneity but made the chiaroscuro more forceful and tightened the dramatic pattern of interlocked stone and timber. The market value of the rare first states is far greater than that of the revised states, but Piranesi surely considered his revisions to be the improvements which art lovers, as distinct from collectors of rarities, have always found them.

(above right)
36 *Carceri d'invenzione*, title-page of the revised edition of c.1761
Etching 54 × 41·4 cm.

(overleaf)
37 *Carceri d'invenzione*, plate two of the revised edition of c.1761
Etching 55·5 × 42 cm.

This etching was one of the new plates in the revised edition of sixteen numbered plates. It is one of the few occasions upon which Piranesi attempted *Grand Guignol* effects of explicit torture, but is none the better for them. Silvia Stewart has pointed out that the inscriptions and effigies record various victims of Nero's rule as documented in the *Annals* of Tacitus. Among them we find 'C. Petronius', Petronius Arbiter, the lyric poet and author of *The Satyricon*. It is noteworthy that Piranesi mis-spelt some proper names, a lapse which smacks of the over-confidence of the self-educated. Someone with no Latin would have been sure to seek a scholar's assistance.

(page 55)
38 *Carceri d'invenzione*, plate eight of the revised edition of c.1761
Etching 54·5 × 40 cm.

There are no significant additions here to the architecture seen in the first state, except the distant vistas faintly described in contrast to the immensely solid foreground masonry. Both solidity and aerial perspective depend upon a chiaroscuro absent in the first state. Much of the impact of the design derives from the absence of any secure horizontal lines to match the massive verticals.

41   *Carceri d'invenzione*, plate fifteen of the revised edition of c.1761
Etching 55×40·5 cm.

The central tablet which here contains a relief of very elongated figures was blank and there were
no bridges and ladders to the left in the first state of this plate. But if there is more detail in the
second version there is, nevertheless, no loss of freedom in execution. The leonine prisoners' heads
remind one of the lions' heads in the *Magnificent Port* (Plate 33). The rings, in any case, resemble
mooring rings and Jonathan Scott has made the interesting suggestion that the canal entrances of
Venetian palaces may have stimulated the conception of the *Carceri* in Piranesi's imagination.

(*opposite top*)
39   *Invenzioni capric di carceri*, plate fourteen
Etching 41×53·5 cm. c.1745–50.

(*opposite bottom*)
40   *Carceri d'invenzione*, plate fourteen of the revised edition of c.1761
Etching 41×53·5 cm.

There are relatively few differences between this plate and the first state: spikes were added to the
timbers in the lower right-hand corner of the revised version, and of course the chiaroscuro was
strengthened, although the faulty perspective was not corrected. To judge by the arch which
connects the pier on the left with that in the centre these piers are on the same plane, but the
staircase suggests that they are on different planes.

42　*Carceri d'invenzione*, plate sixteen of the revised edition of c.1761
Etching 55 × 40·5 cm.

This plate is a complete revision of the first state, with the addition of many more instruments of torture, together with antique references. Sylvia Stewart has suggested that this plate is complementary to the second plate of the revised set (Plate 37), which shows the injustice of Rome under the tyrant Nero. The inscriptions refer to Livy's account of the institution of Roman prisons and thus allude to the true justice of Rome under her first kings. It has also been suggested that Piranesi here committed a Greek doric column to Roman imprisonment, and he certainly did torture it by making the central section of its fluted shaft a size too large. This is just the sort of discordant effect Piranesi relished in the designs of his *Parere su l'architettura* (Plate 68).

(*opposite*)
43　*Staircase before a Vaulted Hall*
LONDON, British Museum (Department of Prints and Drawings). Pen and brown ink with wash over a red chalk sketch 38·2 × 25·5 cm. c.1750–55.

This drawing probably represents an idea for an etching which Piranesi never published. It is this style of drawing which was imitated by Charles Michel-Ange Challe (fig. 12). The idea of the

composition clearly derived from earlier baroque artists (fig. 1), but the extraordinary notion of passing both columns through a massive block has no precedent, nor surely can anyone have ever designed an entablature such as this before Piranesi. The stairs on the left are impeded by a version of the sarcophagus of Cecilia Metella (fig. 5) about eight times larger than the original. A reclining effigy of the Etruscan type appears to repose on top of it. The niche in the lower right of the drawing looks forward to some of the artist's ideas for chimneypieces.

A e B *Veduta degli Avanzi delle Case de Cesari sul Palatino.* C *Avanzi della Casa Augustana.* D *Avanzi della Casa Tiberiana.* E *Avanzi della Casa Neroniana.* F *Luogo ov'era il Circo Massimo.* G *Avanzi delle sostruzioni de Sedili del medesimo Circo.* H *Marana o sia Acqua Crabra.*

Piranesi Archit. dis. e inc.

44   *Antichità romane*, volume one, plate thirty-five, figure one: *the Palatine*
Etching 13·6 × 27·4 cm. c.1752.

The four volumes of *Antichità romane* were published in 1756. The etchings in the first volume of the *Antichità romane* are different from those in the succeeding three volumes and resemble, in scale and format and, to some extent, style, the *Archi trionfali* series (Plates 15 and 16). This view of the Palatine Hill conveys remarkably well the organic continuity that one senses between crumbling buildings and the heaving soil in some parts of Rome.

(opposite top)
45   *Study for the Dedicatory Plate to Volume Two of 'Antichità romane'*
LONDON, British Museum (Department of Prints and Drawings). Pen and brown ink and wash over a sketch in red and black chalk 40 × 63·5 cm. c.1756.

In this as in many other drawings, Piranesi allowed his quill pen to spread under pressure in a way which would have been ruinous had his hand faltered. The wash seems almost to have been spilt onto the paper. In the etching (Plate 46) many more figures were added, together with more detail in the architecture, and the trees were made much more distinct than the vapour-like indications in this drawing. Ruled orthogonals are just evident on top of the drawing of the architecture.

(opposite bottom)
46   *Antichità romane*, volume two, dedicatory plate (second state): *Reconstruction of the Via Appia*
Etching 39·5 × 64 cm. c.1756.

The first state of the etching included tombs inscribed in honour of Piranesi's friends Robert Adam and the Scottish portraitist Allan Ramsay, also one for his patron Lord Charlemont and for Charlemont's agent in Rome, John Parker. The inscription to Parker was struck out in the second state.

VEDUTA degli Avanzi di Fabbrica magnifica sepolcrale co'fue Rovine, la quale si vede vicina a Torre de'Schiavi un miglio e mezzo in circa fuori di Porta Maggiore

49 *Antichità romane*, volume two, plate sixty: *Sepulchral Ruins near Torre di Schiavi*
Etching 47 × 52·5 cm. c.1756.

The Torre di Schiavi was a medieval construction built on top of a Roman mausoleum. The ruins of the third-century villa of the Gordian emperors were also in this area of the Campagna. This etching is an admirable example of the surgical aspect of Piranesi's attitude to ruins and even the trees instruct us as to the thickness of the masonry in which they have taken root. They also, of course, add interest to the silhouette, as does the brilliantly placed goat on the left. The miniature views seen through the building are as delightful as the best of the very early, small *Varie vedute*.

(opposite top)
47 *Antichità romane*, volume three, dedicatory plate (second state): *Reconstruction of a Hippodrome with Part of the Via Appia*
Etching 40 × 60 cm. c.1756.

In the first state of this plate an altar in the foreground was decorated with an inscription to Lord Charlemont. This was replaced with a dedication to Mars the Avenger after Piranesi quarrelled with his patron. The vertiginous drop from the terrace walk on the left never fails to startle even those who are very familiar with this etching. On the right there is a bizarre variation on the theme of the sarcophagus of Cecilia Metella (fig. 5).

(opposite bottom)
48 *Antichità romane*, volume four, dedicatory plate (second state)
Etching 39·5 × 53·8 cm. c.1756.

In the first state there was another inscription to Charlemont, but this too was eliminated and replaced by a dedication to patrons of the arts in general. The composition looks back to that of *A Magnificent Bridge* (Plate 4), but here the vista is interrupted by a screen of columns. These are unfluted, unusual in Piranesi's mature works, because they are evidently single pieces of coloured marble or granite, like the monoliths of the Pantheon, which thrilled seventeenth- and eighteenth-century visitors to Rome.

VEDUTA degli Avanzi... ...mere sepolcrali esistenti sull'antica Via Appia fuori di Porta S. Sebastiano. A Camera di tre Appatamenti, une de quali in ogni rimane so... B Rovine di nobilissima Villa degli antichi Romani. C Selci dell'antica Via Appia. Piranesi Archit. f...

50 *Antichità romane*, volume two, plate forty-seven: *View of the Via Appia*
Etching 37·5 × 51·5 cm. c.1756.

In his caption Piranesi itemized, in addition to the central building and a distant villa, the polygonal paving stones of the Via Appia which he piled up dramatically to the left of the plate. Piranesi developed the chiaroscuro of his plates after he had worked out his composition and one notices that here, before the last biting of the acid, he had to be careful that his shadows did not obscure the staff of a small figure standing to the right.

(opposite top)
51 *Antichità romane*, volume two, plate fifty-seven: *Urns and Cippi from the Villa Corsini*
Etching 37 × 62 cm. c.1756.

Piranesi here provided accurate information about the objects which he illustrated, except that he increased their scale enormously. The calculated contrasts, between the rotten tree trunk, the crumbling rendering of the wall and the marble, between the encrusted ornamentation and the smooth surfaces, between the rotund and the angular, are such as only Piranesi could have contrived. All the same he claimed that the urns and cippi were arranged in this order on a wall of the Casino of the Villa Corsini. The casino, which was destroyed in the nineteenth century, had been built in the late seventeenth century and many ruins were uncovered when the foundations were dug. Such picturesque arrangements of miscellaneous urns, altars and inscriptions were a feature of many Roman courtyards and gardens from the Renaissance onwards.

(opposite bottom)
52 *Antichità romane*, volume three, plate eight: *View of the Via Appia*
Etching 36 × 59 cm. c.1756.

URNE CIPPI E VASI CENERARJ DI MARMO NELLA VILLA CORSINI FUORI DI PORTA S. PANCRAZIO

2

VEDUTA del Lato posteriore del Mausoleo di Cecilia Metella, comunem. detto Capo di Bove, eretto sopra l'antica Via Appia poco lungi dalla Chiesa di S.Sebastiano, fuori delle Mura. Egli
grande, fu demolito in buona parte, e resta ne'tempi miserabile delle discordie tralle principali Famiglie Romane, convertito in Rocca con un Castello accanto. 1 Muro co'merli fabbricato ne'tempi bassi. 2 V

53 *Antichità romane*, volume three, plate fifty-one: *the Mausoleum of Cecilia Metella*
Etching 40 × 60 cm. c.1756.

This building, vulgarly called 'Capo di Bove' after the ox-head ornaments of the frieze, is one of the most impressive mausolea on the Via Appia. It was much admired during the eighteenth century and during the early nineteenth century when Byron wrote his elegiac lines on this ruin in *Childe Harold.* The exquisite marble sarcophagus in the Palazzo Farnese (fig. 5), which so fascinated Piranesi, was found inside the building. A view of the mausoleum was also etched for the *Vedute di Roma.*

54 *Antichità romane*, volume three, plate fifty-three: *the Way in which the Great Blocks of Travertine Were Raised in the Building of the Mausoleum of Cecilia Metella*
Etching 46·5 × 52 cm. c.1756.

Piranesi here reconstructed how wedges were inserted in the tops of some blocks and grappling irons were fitted into the sides of the larger ones. The grappling irons were used in conjunction with spliced loops of rope fastened around projecting knobs of stone. Explanations of technical matters of this sort always need illustrations if they are to be fully grasped, yet Piranesi's illustration is so full and ingenious that he could almost have dispensed with the explanatory prose, given in a separate etched plate immediately below the image.

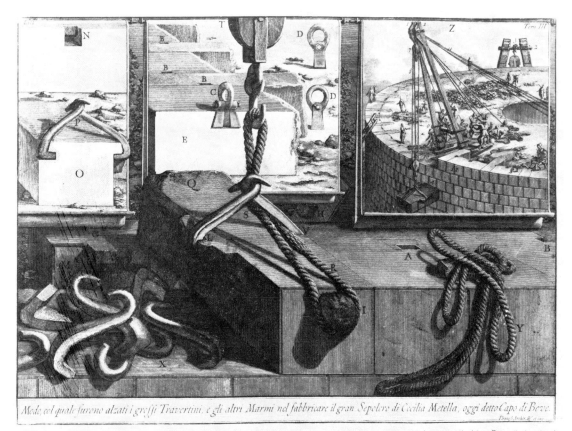

Veduta di una parte de' fondamenti del Teatro di Marcello

A *Palizzate piantate nel terren vergine per sicurezza de' fondamenti* B *Base fondamentale di quattr'ordini di peperini* C D *Speroni, ovvero barbacani* E *Fondamenti interni di opera incerta* F *Cloaca maestra sotto l'ambulacro de portici destinata allo scolo delle im mondezze, e delle acque piovane* G *Una delle cloache sotto i cunei del Teatro destinate al medesimo fine, e corrispondente coll'anzidetta* M *Lastrico dell'ambulacro suddetto* I *Dimostrazione de tre gradi circolari esterni del Teatro, che in cominciavano dal piano antico di Roma* L *Dimostrazione di una parte di uno de pilastri del Teatro*

Reliquiae theatri Marcelli. A.*Rudera porticus retro scenam ipsius theatri.*
B *Ruinæ substructionum graduum spectaculorum.*
Vide indicem ruinarum num 62.

Piranesi F.

56 *Campus Martius*, plate twenty-seven: *the Remains of the Theatre of Marcellus*
Etching 23·2 × 35 cm. c.1762.

The extraordinary power of Piranesi's archaeological imagination is nowhere more evident than in
this plate in which he has shorn from the Roman ruins all modern additions illustrated in the
Vedute di Roma (Plate 25) unless perhaps it is in his reconstruction of the theatre in its original
splendour (Plate 57). Piranesi's *Campus Martius* was published in 1762.

(*opposite*)
55 *Antichità romane*, volume four, plate thirty-two: *Part of the Foundations of the Theatre of Marcellus*
Etching 39·5 × 59 cm. c.1756.

At the very top of the print is the lower part of one of the engaged columns on the ground floor of
the theatre and the three steps surrounding the building. Even these were buried by the mid-
eighteenth century, as we can see from the view of the building in the *Vedute di Roma* (Plate 25),
but Piranesi could easily have excavated that far. He might even have found the drain which is
marked 'F' on the etching, but the remainder of the theatre's foundations, the solid base of blocks
of *peperini* resting on densely packed piles, were hypothetical, although presented with absolute
conviction. In the same volume of *Antichità romane* Piranesi also etched the equally hypothetical
foundations of the Castel Sant' Angelo and its bridge.

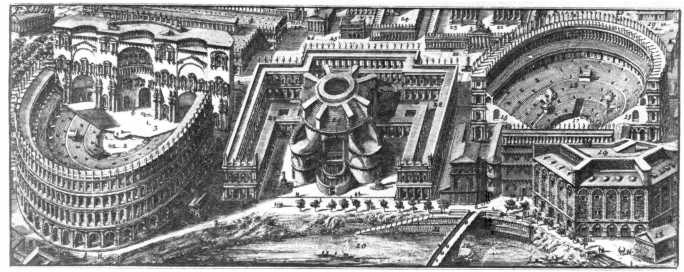

Elevazione de' Teatri di Balbo, e di Marcello con gli altri edifizj ch'eran loro vicini.

Scenographia Theatrorum Balbi, et Marcelli aliorumque aedificiorum, quae prope habuerunt.

Piranesi F.

57 *Campus Martius*, plate forty-eight a: *the Theatres of Balbus and Marcellus and the Neighbouring Architecture*
Etching 11 × 28·7 cm. c.1762.

The Campus Martius, or Field of Mars, was originally an open parade ground and sports field near the Tiber, but it had, by early imperial times, been given over to temples, theatres and baths. The position of these theatres was clear from the antique plan of Rome in the Capitol, but whereas a substantial portion of the Theatre of Marcellus (Plate 25) survives, all that remains of the Theatre of Balbus is a fragment of old wall built into a house in the Via Santa Maria de' Calderari. The Theatre of Balbus was dedicated by L. Cornelius Balbus in 13 B.C. and so was contemporary with the Theatre of Marcellus.

58 *Della magnificenza ed architettura de' Romani*, page three
Etching and the initial letter of the folio text.
c.1761.

The text of *Della magnificenza*, published in 1761, was in both Italian and Latin. For the initial letter of the Italian text Piranesi etched the frowning *Brutus*, a bronze bust thought to be of great antiquity which was to be enormously revered in Revolutionary France and which suited Piranesi's uncompromising polemical attitude in this tract against the hellenists who underestimated Roman civilization.

iii

DELLA
MAGNIFICENZA
ED ARCHITETTURA
DE' ROMANI.

A gran tempo fra me penſando, perchè mai, non eſſendovi chi neghi,aver il popolo Romano fiorito nelle arti della guerra, e della pace, tolgagliſi poi da taluno la lode della magnificenza, m' è ſembrato, ciò derivare da una certa ſoverchia facilità, e precipitanza nel giudicare, quanto in oggi contraria alla riputazion de' Romani, altrettanto nociva ſempre alla verità. Imperocchè negli oggetti medeſimi molte ſono le coſe, che impedir ne ſogliono l' agevole cognizione, e vi ſi aggiugne altreſì alle volte tale traſcorſo di tempo, e tal diverſità di opinioni intorno a quelli, che nulla può eſſer più a propoſito, o anche più ſaggiamente far ſi può,quanto il confeſſar di non ſapere, qual giudizio formar ſe ne debba. Nondimeno cert' uni o allettati dalla dolcezza della novità, o ſtimolati dall'impegno, non per queſto ſi ritengono dal giudicar liberamente di coſe dubbie, i quali io ſtimerei ſopportabili ſe il faceſſero dopo aver, benchè leggiermente,eſaminata la cauſa,poichè ſembrerebbe, che aveſſero avuto qualche riguardo di rintracciare il vero. Or formandoſi da eſſi tali giudizj, che addur non ſanno il motivo de' lor ſentimenti, e proponendoci coſe,non com'elle ſono, ma quali vorrebbon che foſſero, qual luogo può rimanere alla verità, trovandoſi ſpezialmente di quelli, che non per mancanza d'ingegno, ma per l' abominazione che hanno all'incomodo di diſputare, e per non tenere in gran pregio ſì fatte controverſie, ſeguono il parere altrui piuttoſto, che giudicarne eſſi ſteſſi? Coſì addiviene, che molte coſe ſi ſpacciano temerariamente tra 'l volgo, e ciò, che una volta v' è ſtato ſparſo, che che egli ſiaſi,ogni dì più vi ſi radica, e ſi divulga. E certamente non mi farei mai immaginato, che avvenir poteſſe a' Romani, di dover eſſer tacciati di puſillanimi, ed affatto rozzi; poichè, quantunque la maggior parte delle loro opere per l'ingiuria de'tempi e delle guerre ſieno perite, tuttavolta io vedea rimanere ſi in Roma, che per l'Italia monumenti tali della lor magnificenza, che mi ſtupiſco, come mai ciò ſia potuto venire in mente ad alcuno, che qualche coſa abbia udito, o letto. Ma perchè tal concetto han de' Romani coloro, che tutto attribuiſcono a' Greci, e queſta loro opinione ſempre più s' avanza preſſo le nazioni ſtraniere, ho creduto eſſer coſa convenevole alla mia profeſſione l' eſaminare il tutto con un poco più di diligenza; affinchè, riconoſciutoſi il peſo delle ragioni, che militano dall' una parte, e dall' altra, rieſca più facile ai giuſti eſtimatori delle coſe il riſolvere, qual giudizio dar ſi debba in queſta cauſa.

I. DUE ragioni veggo addurſi da coloro, che invidiano, o, ſe non altro, non favoriſcono la gloria de' Romani; per le quali queſti, prima di ſoggiogar la Grecia, furon privi, com' eſſi dicono, di qualſivoglia magnificenza di opere; cioè, la povertà, e l'ignoranza di tutte le arti della pace. Per dir qualche coſa intorno alla povertà, ſi fa da autori di credito, ch' e' non moſſero guerra ai Greci, ſe non dopo aver ſottomeſſa l' Italia; il che non eſſendoſi fatto con una ſola ſcorreria di ſoldati, ma col traſcorſo d'un lungo tempo, qual coſa mai li trattenne, che a mano a mano non s' arricchiſſero colle ſpoglie degl' Italiani? Poichè non eran mica poveri, come forſe talun penſa, gl' Italiani, eſſendo abitatori d' un paeſe de' più felici⁽²⁾, e di più provvedendo colle loro arti ed induſtria in ſì fatta guiſa al loro privati biſogni, e al decoro della repubblica,che,ſecondo la condizione di que' tempi,non la cedevano a verun'altra nazione. Or non avendo i Romani guerreggiato con forte avverſa,nè ſofferto ſterilità de'campi, per qual motivo pretendono alcuni,ch'e' foſſer poveri,e che perciò non aveſſero potuto innalzar fabbrica da vantarſene?

(1) Dionigi nel lib. 1. delle antich. Rom.   a 2   Sem-

70

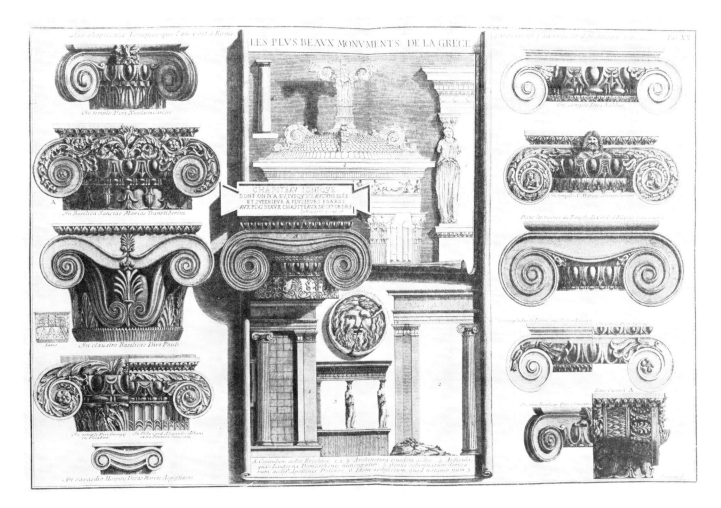

59 *Della magnificenza ed architettura de' Romani*, plate twenty: *Roman and Greek Ionic Capitals*
Etching 39 × 59 cm. 1761.

Piranesi copied two pages from Le Roy's hellenistic *Les plus beaux monuments de la Grèce* in this etching, illustrating accurately Le Roy's representation of the beautiful ionic capital of the Erechtheum on the Athenian Acropolis, but then surrounding it with other ionic capitals, all but one of which were from Roman buildings which, he believed, displayed the superior inventiveness of the Romans. Piranesi was fighting a losing battle. For most of his contemporaries and for the following generations the two most beautiful ionic capitals were those of the Erechtheum, shown in the centre of Piranesi's etching, and of the Temple of Ceres on the Illisus, shown in the centre on the right, and both of them are Greek.

(overleaf)
60 *Vedute di Roma*: the Temple of the Sybil, Tivoli
Etching 62 × 43·5 cm. c.1761.

A full archaeological survey of this temple, perhaps projected by Piranesi in the 1760s, was actually carried out by his son Francesco and published in 1780 as *Raccolta de' tempi antichi. Opera di Francesco Piranesi prime parte…* By placing such emphasis on its substructure Piranesi made the elegant little temple look far grander than it is in reality. Few works of antiquity were more loved in the eighteenth century than the Temple of the Sybil. Confining our attention to the English we find Richard Wilson painting numerous landscapes in which the temple is the principal attraction, Dance reverently measuring it, the Earl of Bristol planning to remove it to Britain, Soane adapting it for a corner of the screen wall of the Bank of England, and Uvedale Price and Payne Knight quarrelling over the vocabulary most proper for describing its charms. The Temple of the Sybil is now known as the Temple of Vesta.

(page 73)
61 *Vedute di Roma*: the Tempio della Tosse
Etching 55 × 62·3 cm. c.1764.

This 'temple', octagonal on the outside and circular within, was converted for Christian worship in late antiquity, but is now believed to have been built as the vestibule of a grand villa. It is situated on the plain below Tivoli. Piranesi's etching includes, in addition to the artist's signature in the bottom right-hand corner, the price of 'paoli due e mezzo', subsequently erased from the bottom left-hand corner in the posthumous state published in Paris. This was Piranesi's standard charge for a single print in the *Vedute di Roma* series, and it was very little. His profit came from a large sale at a low individual price, which was probably necessary to discourage rivals. Piranesi claimed that he took 4000 impressions from each plate. Half of that would have been a remarkable yield from a copper plate.

Veduta interna del Tempio della Tosse costruito di materi di tufi, e Muri, ed quali erano state murate le finestre ne'tempi bassi.

Rovine d'una Galleria
di Statue nella Villa Adri
ana a Tivoli
A. Avanzi di pitture a grottesco.

63 *Vedute di Roma*: Hadrian's Villa, the Canopus
Etching 44·5 × 58 cm. c.1769.

Hadrian's gigantic, sprawling retreat at Tivoli, built between A.D. 125 and 134 consisted of
buildings intended to evoke the different styles and different periods of architecture and the
different religions which the restless emperor had admired when touring Greece, Asia Minor and
Egypt. The Canopus was inspired by the Temple of Serapis near Alexandria. In front of it was a
canal, restored in the twentieth century, which reflected in its waters replicas of classical statuary.
Hadrian's Villa had been excavated during the sixteenth and seventeenth centuries, but the most
spectacular finds were made in the eighteenth century, many by Piranesi himself. The symmetry of
this composition and also that of *The Tempio della Tosse* (Plate 61), almost inevitable considering the
character of the buildings portrayed, was anticipated in Piranesi's early small views of the Temple
of Venus and the Baths of Titus.

(*preceding page*)
62 *Vedute di Roma*: Hadrian's Villa, Ruins of the Statue Gallery
Etching 45·5 × 58 cm. c.1770.

This building is now known to have been the central room of the larger *thermae*, or baths, rather
than the statue gallery. Piranesi indicated with the letter 'A', near the upper left-hand corner, the
part of the vault which retained some remains of antique 'grotesque' painting. The festoons of
foliage are as delightfully varied and as delicate as frost patterns on glass.

64 *Young Man Gesticulating*
OXFORD, Ashmolean Museum. Pen and brown ink
16 × 10 cm. c.1761.

This long-armed scarecrow is typical of the figures which
populate Piranesi's prints and which surely owe as much
to the seventeenth-century paintings of Salvator Rosa as
they do to Piranesi's observations of life. This sketch was
dashed down on the verso of part of a proof impression of
the twelfth plate of *Della magnificenza*, the publication of
which in 1761 probably dates this sheet to the early
1760s. It is easy to imagine that Piranesi had a supply of
such figures which he fitted into his etchings with
decreasing regard for narrative connections.

**65 *Emissario del Lago Albano*: *Plan, Cross-section, Map and
Views of the Entrance of the Tunnel***
Etching 40·5 × 50·5 cm. c.1762.

Lake Albano, one of the most celebrated landmarks
around Rome, is contained in a long-exhausted crater.
The Romans, prompted by an oracle according to Livy,
drove a tunnel through the hill in order to drain part of
the lake, a feat of engineering which fascinated Piranesi.
This etching provides a good example of Piranesi's skill at
packing information into his plates in a way which is as
exciting as it is economical of space. It also neatly
illustrates the limits of his reliability. His discovery of the
outlets from the tunnel into the hillside above and his
surveying in general are thorough, but the actual tunnel
entrance does not match his sublime representation of it
in the inset view here. Piranesi's *Emissario del Lago Albano*
was published in 1762.

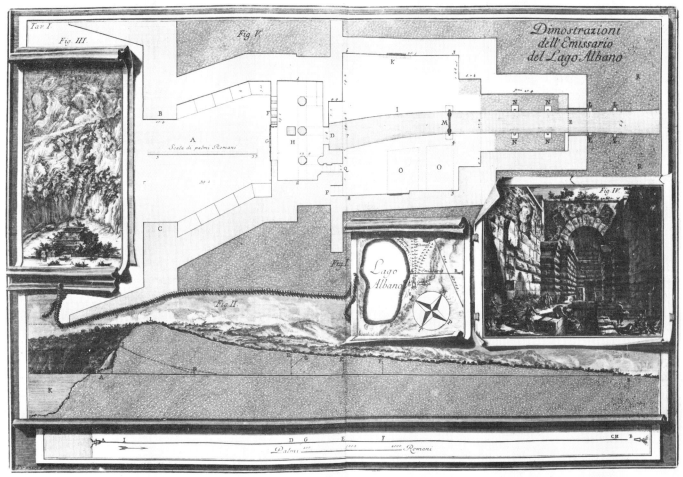

66 *Emissario del Lago Albano*: *the Entrance of the Tunnel*
Etching 45 × 64 cm. c.1762.

This etching shows the innermost area of the tunnel entrance depicted in the inset view of the introductory plan, cross-section and map (Plate 65), although the tree trunks which make so striking an appearance here are not present there. This difference between the two etchings is tantamount to an admission on the artist's part that he took as much licence with vegetation as with humans in his topographical work.

Elevazione e prospetto d'un'altra piscina esistente nella vigna
de PP della Compagnia di Gesù a Castel Gandolfo

67   *Antichità d'Albano e di Castel Gandolfo: Cistern near Castel Gandolfo*
Etching 40·5 × 61·5 cm. c.1764.

The *Antichità d'Albano*, published in 1764, was dedicated to Pope Clement XIII Rezzonico and
completed at his special behest. The Venetian pope knighted Piranesi and made him papal
antiquary and, according to Legrand, the two men were intimates, Clement even consulting the
artist over international pressure on him to suppress the Jesuit Order. This ruin was situated in a
vineyard belonging to the Jesuits near the pope's summer retreat at Castel Gandolfo. Piranesi never
surpassed the range of tone, the dramatic perspective and the rendering of the slanting light of this
etching, which, in some ways, is a less agitated equivalent of the fourteenth plate of the *Carceri*
(Plate 40).

68 *Parere su l'architettura: Architectural Fantasy*
Etching 39 × 54 cm. c.1765.

The quotation from Le Roy to the effect that the sublime
art of architecture should not be made a matter of slavish
copying is ironic. Piranesi was violently opposed to the
hellenistic French theorist and knew that Le Roy, whilst
appealing to the imagination, could not possibly have
approved of such an extreme architectural fantasy as this
one. Piranesi had detected the trend in neo-classical
architecture which culminated in England with the
success of learned but unimaginative architects such as
Wilkins and in the text of *Parere*, published in 1765, and
plates such as this, he reacted violently against pedantry.
All the same, parts of this bizarre composition are correct
quotations from the antique; the griffins were taken from
the frieze of the Temple of Antoninus and Faustina in
the Forum and the spirally fluted columns to the
door were very common on Roman sarcophagi, Piranesi
considering this type of fluting to have been an Etruscan
invention. There were also numerous prototypes for the
knotted dolphins, although no antique Roman relief
carving made them look so much like hemp. It seems
unlikely that Piranesi intended this design to be taken
entirely seriously. Every part was devised to seem
shockingly out of scale with a neighbouring part, as in
some perverse architectural game.

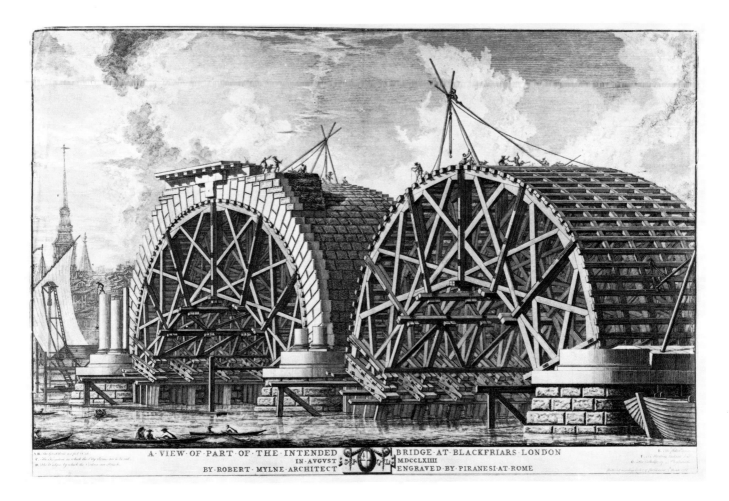

A·VIEW·OF·PART·OF·THE·INTENDED BRIDGE·AT·BLACKFRIARS·LONDON IN·AVGVST MDCCLXIIII
BY·ROBERT·MYLNE·ARCHITECT ENGRAVED·BY·PIRANESI·AT·ROME

70   *Blackfriars Bridge*
Etching 37 × 60 cm. 1766.

This view of the centring of one of London's new bridges in 1764 was published on its own on 10 March 1766 and was etched for the bridge's architect Robert Mylne, whom Piranesi had befriended in Rome, where Mylne had won first prize in the Concorso Clementino. Mylne acted as Piranesi's London agent when he returned to Britain. The bridge was opened in 1769. Although Mylne's architecture is not, in general, Piranesian, this bridge was a modest version of the design for *A Magnificent Bridge* (Plate 4) in Piranesi's *Prima parte* etchings. Piranesi also etched some of Adam's work at Syon House and it cannot but have struck him how speedily the young British architects whom he knew in Rome found employment on their return home. No wonder he is said to have declared that if he left Rome it would only be to come to London. Appropriately, the letters 'S.P.Q.L.', standing for 'Senatus Populus Que Londiniensis', are shown with the city arms in the title, an inescapable allusion to the letters 'S.P.Q.R.', which appeared on all Roman public works.

(opposite bottom)
69   *Parere su l'architettura*: the Projected Temple for the Society of Antiquaries, London
Etching 16 × 21·5 cm. c.1765.

Piranesi was elected a member of the Society of Antiquaries, London, in 1757 on account of his *Antichità romane*, whereas he was only elected to the academy of Roman artists, the Accademia di San Luca, four years later in 1761. He was very conscious of the honour of belonging to the Society of Antiquaries and in this print projected new premises for its members. By Piranesi's standards the frieze of griffins and the reliefs of the Muses, in both the central element and the pediment and surrounding the lower parts of the conical obelisks, are unusually elegant. And this makes the monstrous, top-heavy composition even more shocking.

(overleaf)
71   *Vedute di Roma*: the Interior of the Basilica of San Giovanni in Laterano
Etching 42·5 × 67·5 cm. c.1768.

This view shows the remodelling of the nave of San Giovanni in Laterano, carried out by Borromini in the late 1640s for which a sanctuary commissioned from Piranesi was to have provided a fitting climax. The soffits of the arches separating nave from aisles are decorated with alternating types of garland which Borromini continued 'through' the capitals of his pilasters, an idea adopted by Piranesi in his projects for the sanctuary of the basilica (Plates 72 and 73).

Veduta interna della Basilica
di S. Giovanni Laterano

83

72   *Design for the Sanctuary of the Basilica of San Giovanni in Laterano*
NEW YORK, Columbia University, Avery Architectural Library. Pen and grey ink over pencil with
grey wash and some brown ink 58·7 × 89·8 cm. 1765–67.

This longitudinal section, the eighth ('Tavola Ottava') in a series of presentation drawings, shows
the south wall of the sanctuary with the transept and part of Borromini's nave. It forms, together
with 'Tavola Decima' (Plate 73) and 'Tavola Vigesimaquinta' (Plate 74), three illustrations of the
most extravagant of the several projects which Piranesi presented for alterations to San Giovanni in
Laterano. He here proposed raising the sanctuary roof in two stages, which would have been a
considerable technical feat. To the left of the drawing Borromini's nave can be seen and Piranesi's
concern to harmonize his own designs with the existing nave is obvious. He had, in any case, a
keen sympathy with Borromini, a fact deplored by James Barry who described Piranesi's 'gusto of
architecture' as 'flowing out of the same cloaca with Borromini's, and other hare-brained moderns'.

(*above left*)
73 *Design for the Sanctuary of the Basilica of San Giovanni in Laterano*
NEW YORK, Columbia University, Avery Architectural Library. Pen and grey ink over pencil with some brown ink 87·6 × 56·4 cm. 1765–67.

This elevation, the tenth ('Tavola Decima') of the presentation drawings, looks east showing the colonnade separating the ambulatory from the presbytery and represents the view taken from the extreme right of the 'Tavola Ottava' (Plate 72). The garlands which circle the round clerestory windows are then passed 'through' the entablature into the massive piers. The way that the drawing is presented as a fictive sheet, curling up at top and bottom and held down with a group of garlands, ribbons, dolphins, eagles' wings and serpents, is reminiscent of some of the elements in Piranesi's much earlier *Grotteschi* (Plates 12 and 13).

(*above right*)
74 *Design for the Sanctuary of the Basilica of San Giovanni in Laterano*
NEW YORK, Columbia University, Avery Architectural Library. Pen and brown ink over pencil with brown and grey washes 90·3 × 72·3 cm. 1765–67.

The twenty-fifth presentation drawing ('Tavola Vigesimaquinta') shows the colonnade separating the ambulatory from the presbytery which is also depicted in 'Tavola Ottava' (Plate 72) and 'Tavola Decima' (Plate 73), but with an alternative design for the attic shown on the left. The play with swags and shells and the capitals incorporating cherubim were both inspired by Borromini's architecture. The rich relief ornament in the frieze would have had to have been undercut to an extraordinary degree to obtain the effect Piranesi wanted.

(above left)
75 Santa Maria del Priorato, Rome, façade
1764–67.

The Church of Santa Maria del Priorato represents the only major architectural project fully realized by Piranesi. The commission included the erection of a new façade and the creation of a new interior scheme for Santa Maria del Priorato, originally built in 1568 as the church of the Knights of Malta, and, indeed, it is Piranesi's façade which is the only part of the exterior possessing any architectural interest. Piranesi's façade originally included an attic above the pediment, but it was removed in the middle of the nineteenth century and to judge from an old drawing it made the façade top-heavy. The width of the front and the size of the entrance were determined by the original church. The pilasters, like those inside the church, have bizarre capitals incorporating representations of a fortress, the emblem of the Rezzonico family, to which both Clement XIII and his nephew, Cardinal Giovanni Battista Rezzonico, Grand Prior of the Knights of Malta, belonged. As it strikes the church, sunlight is broken by the dense ornament and by the mouldings and flutings into a pattern of almost mesmeric complexity.

(above right)
76 Santa Maria del Priorato, Rome, interior
1764–67.

Wittkower pointed out how the articulation of this interior, the varied treatment of the order, the way that the altar rails are advanced into the nave and also the special lighting of the apse, are characteristic of northern Italian, and especially Venetian, architecture. The altar itself was certainly Piranesi's invention but the figure of the ecstatic St. Basil above it was perhaps partly the invention of Tommaso Righi who was the chief statuary employed.

(above left)
77   Santa Maria del Priorato, Rome, central stucco panel of the vaulting
1764–67.

The account book for the rebuilding of Santa Maria del Priorato is preserved in the Avery
Architectural Library, Columbia University, New York, and describes this panel in detail.
In the centre is an equilateral triangle, symbolic of the Trinity and composed of rose garlands.
Supported by angels and surrounded by clouds is the Cross and around this we see the shields,
ships' prows and the shirt of the Knights of Malta. Detailed drawings in the Pierpont Morgan
Library, New York, show that the design of this was entirely by Piranesi, although it was executed
by Tommaso Righi. The ornament derives both from the antique, as in the rostral ornaments and
trophies, and from the baroque, for instance the pancake clouds and the rays of glory.

(above right)
78   Santa Maria del Priorato, Rome, niche in the south side of the nave
1764–67.

One of Piranesi's chief tasks in redesigning the interior of the church of the Knights of Malta was
to accommodate a number of important tombs, ranging in style from the romanesque to the
baroque. Each one was placed in a shallow niche decorated with such tact that no tomb seems out
of place. Some niches were left empty, and in this one Piranesi's own tomb was erected in 1779
when his remains, buried at first in Sant' Andrea delle Frate, were moved to Santa Maria del
Priorato. The tomb takes the form of a statue by Giuseppe Angelini showing the artist clad in
classical robes and in a pensive attitude, leaning on a herm. The stucco decoration behind,
designed by Piranesi, is much more exciting.

(above left)
79   *Diverse maniere: Designs for Coffee-pots, Clock-cases, a Sedan-chair, a Console Table and a Coach*
Etching 38·5 × 25·2 cm. c.1769.

In *Diverse maniere*, published in 1769, Piranesi stressed the licence which it was legitimate for the creative artist to exercise, in particular when inventing ornament for objects which did not exist in antiquity, such as coffee-pots, clock-cases and chimneypieces. Looking back, perhaps to his own youthful flirtation with the rococo style, he recommended the modern decorator to take hints from sea shells. Piranesi perhaps knew that the hellenist Winckelmann in his *Reflections on the Imitation of the Painting and Sculpture of the Greeks* of 1756 had made a special point of objecting to shell ornament, as he also objected, as had Vitruvius, to much Roman 'grotesque' decoration.

(above right)
80   *Diverse maniere: Design for a Chimneypiece, a Mirror and 'Grotesque' Decoration*
Etching 33·5 × 24·5 cm. c.1769.

The 'grotesque' decoration here is derived from the so-called 'fourth style' Roman wall painting and shallow stucco work. Piranesi illustrated Roman 'grotesque' decoration in the section of volume two of his *Antichità romane* devoted to the tomb of L. Arruntius, and he also drew attention to traces of it which survived in Hadrian's Villa (Plate 63). The style was taken up in France in the 1770s by Jean Dugourc in his interiors for Bélanger's Bagatelle.

(opposite top)
81   Chimneypiece
AMSTERDAM, Rijksmuseum. Marble. c.1765.

This superbly carved chimneypiece was published in the *Diverse maniere* as one that had been executed for John Hope of Amsterdam, father of Thomas Hope, the important promoter of English neo-classicism. Piranesi claimed in the caption that the architrave and 'other pieces' of marble were antique. Certainly there were antique prototypes for many of the ornaments and also for the hovering smiles on the faces of the terminal fauns.

(opposite bottom)
82   *Diverse maniere: Design for a Chimneypiece in the Egyptian Manner*
Etching 24·5 × 38 cm. c.1769.

Although elements of Egyptian decoration had been employed by earlier European artists,

especially for tombs, Piranesi seems to have been the first designer to recommend the domestication of the Egyptian style and the first to design Egyptian chimneypieces of the type which were to become highly fashionable in England, France and Italy during the first decade of the nineteenth century. Piranesi believed that Roman civilization stemmed from Egypt rather than from Greece and he would also have known that the earliest revival of Egyptian decoration was by the Romans, in particular by the Emperor Hadrian, whose villa at Tivoli he not only etched but also excavated.

Pare spaccato per longo della stessa bottega, ove si vedono fra le aperture del vestibolo le immense piramide, ed altri edifizj sepolcrali ne' deserti dell' Egitto.

83   *Diverse maniere: Decoration for the Caffè degli Inglesi, Piazza di Spagna, Rome*
Etching 21 × 32 cm. c.1767.

These designs for the Caffè degli Inglesi were certainly completed by 1767, although *Diverse maniere*, in which they were included, was not published until two years later. There is no need to suppose that Piranesi actually painted the decoration of the coffee house himself, any more than that he carved the chimneypieces he sold at this period. Indeed, although the plate is signed by Piranesi, this need not indicate that even the etching was by him, for he stated in the text of *Diverse maniere*, which was published in English and French as well as in Italian, that 'the graver and the aqua fortis have not been so obedient to the Ingraver as the Architect could have wished'. The coffee house was no doubt too confined for Piranesi to have effectively extended its architectural dimensions, and so he designed screens of Egyptian architecture parallel to the wall plane and he permitted glimpses of the Egyptian landscape beyond. This decorative scheme represented a key moment in the progress of Egyptian revival, but it seems that Piranesi took the style less seriously than did those architects who employed it later to provide an imposing setting for Napoleon I, or to adorn suburban cemeteries or triumphs of heavy engineering. Piranesi's locusts and crocodile are as intentionally comic as they would have been in an early twentieth-century cinema, and he denied that the Egyptian ornament was laden with arcane meanings. He considered it as whimsical nonsense, comparable to *chinoiserie*.

84   Chimneypiece
SCOTLAND, Wedderburn Castle. White marble with amethyst cameos and relief panels of *rosso antico*.
c.1774.

This chimneypiece was admired by Father Thorpe, the Jesuit agent of the Earl of Arundel, in the spring of 1774, but before he could acquire it for Wardour Castle, Patrick Home bought it for 371 scudi for Wedderburn Castle, Berwickshire, where it was recently identified by Alistair Rowan. Wedderburn was then being erected to designs by Robert and James Adam. The interiors are not by the Adam brothers, but this chimneypiece has an elegance which is at once worthy of the Adams at their best and unexpected in Piranesi. Other of Piranesi's chimneypieces, those, for instance, at Burghley and at Gorhambury, also reflect the eighteenth-century passion for the coloured marbles, the porphyry and the granites of antiquity.

85 *The Warwick Vase*

WARWICK, Warwick Castle. Marble 1·70 m. high; 2·11 m. in diameter; 81·5 gallons capacity. Early second century A.D.

This magnificent vase was discovered by Gavin Hamilton in a lake which he and Piranesi had drained at Hadrian's Villa in the winter of 1770–71. It was patched up in Piranesi's workshop, the foot being added, according to Michaelis, and given pride of place in his publication *Vasi, candelabri, cippi* … Sir William Hamilton bought *The Warwick Vase* and brought it to England in 1774 and from him it passed to George Greville, Earl of Warwick. The celebrity of this antique was reflected by Paul Storr's reduced copies of the vase in silver and by the full-size bronze copies cast by Thomason of Birmingham, one of which is to be seen in front of the Senate House at Cambridge, just as the renown of *The Portland Vase* was reflected in Wedgwood's imitations. Piranesi expatiated with understandable enthusiasm on the carving and on the inventive design, on the vitality of the twisted handles which turn into delicate vine sprays and on the ingenious use of the panther skin.

(*above left*)
86 Candelabrum
OXFORD, Ashmolean Museum. Marble c.1·83 m. high. c.1775.

This is one of two candelabra etched for *Vasi, candelabri, cippi . . .* and purchased in 1775 by Sir Roger Newdigate for 1000 scudi. Richard Hayward, a London sculptor and both a restorer of and dealer in antiques, provided the plinths in 1776, and in 1777 Newdigate presented the candelabra to the University of Oxford as ornaments for the Radcliffe Camera. Perhaps only someone whose taste for the antique was founded on a study of works such as the *Magnificent Port* (Plate 33) could have thought this to be anything other than an invention of Piranesi's. Even so, the Oxford candelabra were composed by Piranesi chiefly of pieces found in his excavations around Tivoli. There are three similarly 'composed' but far less interesting candelabra in the Lady Lever Art Gallery, Port Sunlight, from Thomas Hope's collection, and there are others in Rome and in the Louvre, Paris, most notably the one (Plate 87) illustrated as the one-hundred-and-eighth plate of *Vasi, candelabri, cippi . . .*

(*above right*)
87 *Vasi, candelabri, cippi . . .,* plate one-hundred-and-eight: *Candelabrum*
Etching 63·5 × 40·5 cm. c.1778.

We must not assume that Piranesi threw his 'composed' candelabra (Plate 86) together as something which could easily be palmed off on a gullible *milord*. Newdigate was, after all, a scholar whom Piranesi respected. Similarly, the 'composed' candelabrum portrayed in this etching from *Vasi, candelabri, cippi . . .,* published as a collection in 1778, was a creation of which Piranesi was immensely proud. The candelabrum itself, even larger than the Oxford candelabra, now adorns the room of antique bronzes in the Louvre. Piranesi assembled it from pieces once *dimessi* or neglected in the Palazzo Salviati at Longara and had intended it for his own monument planned at one time for the Chiesa della Certosa. The Louvre candelabrum is shown behind the artist in the portrait of Piranesi by P. Labruzzi, now in the Museo di Roma. Piranesi's children, Francesco, Pietro and Laura, as well as continuing the family business in prints, were also involved in the manufacture of antique replicas in *terre étrusque* at the Napoleonic factory at Plailly, near Mortefontaine. A training in their father's sculpture workshop would have helped them with this endeavour.